Classical World Series

ATHENS AND SPARTA

S.C. Todd
///

Bristol Classical Press

General Editor: John H. Betts
Series Editor: Michael Gunningham

DF214
.T63
1996x

First published in 1996 by
Bristol Classical Press
an imprint of
Gerald Duckworth & Co. Ltd
48 Hoxton Square
London N1 6PB

© 1996 by S.C. Todd

All rights reserved. No part of this publication
may be reproduced, stored in a retrieval system, or
transmitted, in any form or by any means, electronic,
mechanical, photocopying, recording or otherwise,
without the prior permission of the publisher.

A catalogue record for this book
is available from the British Library

ISBN 1-85399-398-0

Available in USA and Canada from:
Focus Information Group
PO Box 369
Newburyport
MA 01950

Printed in Great Britain by
The Cromwell Press Ltd., Melksham, Wiltshire

Table of Contents

NOV 06

List of Illustrations

Preface

The Classical World Series seeks to look at major topics from a wide-ranging perspective. The aim of this book is to explore two societies which came into direct conflict in the so-called Peloponnesian War (431-404 BC), but its chronological scope is much wider than that: events both earlier and later are discussed because of the way that they contribute to shaping our image of the two societies. A Chronological Table is included at the start of the book, to help set in context the various events that are mentioned.

The writer of any book incurs many debts. My thanks are due to the series editor, Michael Gunningham, for asking me to contribute this volume, and for his patience, support and encouragement when I eventually began to write it. The wide range of this book has involved me in a number of topics about which I know little, and I would like to thank various colleagues in Keele and elsewhere: Paul Cartledge, Andrew Fear, and Robin Osborne read the whole manuscript, and Stephen Hodkinson and Alison Sharrock read bits of it. Each of them has helped to reduce my ignorance and to sharpen my thoughts. Andrew Burgess, Jan Jordan, Jim McCartney, Ron Stroud, Richard Wallace, and Sheila Walton helped me to gather and prepare illustrations. But my greatest debt is to successive groups of Greek History students at Keele over the past eight years, who have allowed me to explore with them ways of studying the subject.

S. C. Todd
University of Keele
August 1995

Chronological Table

For many of the earlier events in this table, the dates given are traditional approximations. It is often particularly difficult to attribute precise dates to ancient authors. The dates given below are meant to indicate general location or duration of literary career, rather than precise life-span.

Archaic Period: conventionally from mid-eighth century to the Persian invasion			
Dates	**Writers**	**At Sparta**	**At Athens**
c. 720, c. 670		Conquest of Messenia	
c. 650	Tyrtaios		
c. 630	Alkman		
590s (or 570s)			Reforms of Solon
c. 570		Battle of the Fetters [if it happened]	
550s to 510s			Tyranny of Peisistratids
c. 520-c. 490		Reign of Kleomenes I	
c. 510			Reforms of Cleisthenes
490			Punitive Persian Raid at Marathon
480-479		Persian Invasion	Persian Invasion

Classical Period: conventionally from the Persian invasion to Alexander's death			
Dates	**Writers**	**At Sparta**	**At Athens**
478-435			Thucydides' *pentêkontaëtia*
460s		Earthquake and helot revolt	
460s			Ephialtes' reforms and full democracy
c. 461-c. 446		The 'First' Peloponnesian War	The 'First' Peloponnesian War
454			League treasury moved to Athens
449			Peace of Kallias [if it happened]
447-438			Building of Parthenon
c. 430s	Herodotus		
c. 430-c. 400	Thucydides		
c. 430-c. 390	Aristophanes		
431-422		Peloponnesian War stage 1: the Arkhidamian War	Peloponnesian War stage 1: the Arkhidamian War
429			Plague, death of Pericles
early 420s [disputed]	Ps.-Xenophon/ Old Oligarch		

Date	Writers	At Sparta	At Athens
425		Pylos: 120 Spartiates captured	Pylos: 120 Spartiates captured
424			Fall of Amphipolis, exile of Thucydides
422		Peace of Nicias	Peace of Nicias
415			Herms and Mysteries scandals
415-413			Expedition to Sicily fails
413-404		Peloponnesian War stage 2: the Ionian/ Dekeleian War	Peloponnesian War stage 2: the Ionian/ Dekeleian War
411			Oligarchy of Four Hundred
410			Democracy restored
404		Surrender of Athens	Surrender of Athens
404/3			Oligarchy of Thirty
403/2			Democracy restored, Amnesty
c. 400-360		Reign of Agesilaos II	
c. 400-c. 355	Xenophon		
c. 400		Spartans invade Asia	

Dates	Writers	At Sparta	At Athens
c. 400		Kinadon's conspiracy	
399			Trial of Socrates
395-387		Corinthian War	Corinthian War
377			Charter of Second Confederacy
371		Battle of Leuktra	
369		Megalopolis and Messene established	
c. 360-322	Aristotle		
357-355			'Social' War
c.355-c. 324			Financial reforms of Euboulos and Lycurgus
338			Philip of Macedon defeats Thebes and Athens at Chaeronea
336-323		Alexander conquers Persian Empire	Alexander conquers Persian Empire
Hellenistic Period: conventionally from Alexander's death to the Roman conquest			
322			Macedonians abolish democracy after Athenian revolt
244-241		Reign of Agis IV	

Date	Writers	At Sparta	At Athens
235-222		Reign of Kleomenes III	
c. 207-192		Tyranny of Nabis	
188		Philopoimen abolishes the *agôgê*	
c. 170-c. 120	Polybius		

Roman Period: conventionally from the sack of Corinth in 146 BC

Date	Writers	At Sparta	At Athens
146		Romans abolish Achaean League, *agôgê* restored	
c. 80-43	Cicero		
c. 60-c. 30	Diodoros		
31 BC - AD 14		Reign of Emperor Augustus: visits Sparta	Reign of Emperor Augustus
c. 30 BC - AD 17	Livy		
c. 80-c. 120	Plutarch		
117-138		Reign of Emperor Hadrian: visits Sparta	Reign of Emperor Hadrian: visits Athens
c. 150	Pausanias		
c. 200-c. 230	Dio Cassius		

Chapter 1:
The Ideal City?

City, State, and Polis

When we talk about ancient Greek history, we think instinctively of Athens and of Sparta, and it is the image of these two communities which forms the subject of this book. Athens, for us, is the world's first democracy and the model on which modern systems of government claim to be based. Sparta is its opposite: the ideal military state, or perhaps the prototype of the British boarding school.

In reality, however, Sparta and Athens were two Greek cities among several hundred others. The nation-state is a modern invention, and there was in antiquity no such country as Greece. There was a Greek language, and it was language which was the principal signifier of Greek identity: so much so that the term 'barbarian' was used to denote non-Greeks, because they made what the Greeks regarded as 'bar-bar' sounds, instead of speaking a proper language. In the fifth and fourth centuries BC, the Greek language was spoken throughout an area roughly corresponding to modern Greece, but not precisely. Northern Greece today includes the regions of Thrace and of Macedonia, but in antiquity Thrace was wholly outside the Greek world, and the status of Macedon was marginal. On the other hand, there were substantial and long-established Greek communities particularly on the coastline of Western Turkey (Ionia) and the Black Sea, and in Southern Italy and Sicily. This latter area, indeed, was known to the Romans under the significant title of *Magna Graecia* or 'Great Greece'.

Language was by no means the only thing that Greek communities had in common. Greeks who wished to appeal to a wider sense of solidarity (as the Athenians do when addressing the Spartans in Herodotus 8.144) could speak of a unity of blood, and of shared customs and religious shrines. But there were also major distinctions. It was not simply the fact (noted at Herodotus 1.56) that Sparta was a Dorian city, whereas Athens could be described as Ionian. (This was fundamentally a linguistic division, in that Dorian and Ionian are the two most prominent among the half-dozen or so dialect-groups into which Greek is conventionally divided, but it may correspond to an underlying division

1

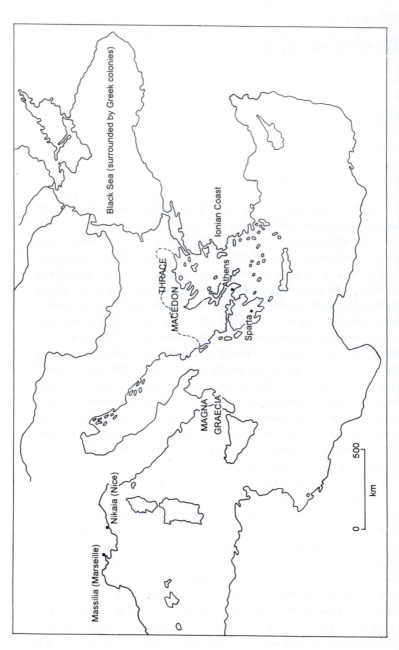

Fig. 1 The Geographical Spread of the Ancient Greek World. [Note the spread of Greek communities around the coasts of much of the Mediterranean. (Nice and Marseille were originally Greek cities.) The dotted line indicates Modern Greece, for comparison.]

between ethnic sub-groups.) More important was the fact that Athens and Sparta were two among many independent *poleis*.

The word *polis* (pl. *poleis*) cannot easily be translated, but it is fundamental to the study of ancient Greece. The nearest English word is 'city', but this masks the fact that the *polis* included not simply an urban centre but also and equally the surrounding countryside. Moreover, whereas most modern cities are little more than centres of local administration, the Greek *polis* was an independent state (hence the conventional if awkward gloss 'city-state'). Each *polis* had its own public officials, its own laws, its own calendar, and the right to mint its own coinage.

Athens in Greek Literature

Most of our evidence for ancient Greek history – at least down to the Macedonian conquest under Philip and Alexander, which ushered in the Hellenistic world – concerns the so-called Classical period: that is, from the defeat of the Persian invasion of 480-479 to Alexander's death in 323 BC. (For the terms Archaic, Classical, and Hellenistic, see the Chronological Table at the start of the book.) The history of Classical Greece is dominated by Athens and Sparta, and at its heart lies the great conflict between the two that we call the Peloponnesian War (431-404 BC).

It would be wrong to assume that Sparta and Athens had at all times been dominant powers within the Greek world. Corinth was always a major *polis*. Argos had at times in the Archaic period been as powerful as Sparta, if not more so. Thebes was an almost-first-rank power, which was to spring into prominence in the first half of the fourth century. Moreover, although the dominance of Sparta was long established, so much so that in 480 BC there could be no question about its right to command the united Greek resistance to Persia, the power of Athens was a more recent phenomenon.

The growing importance of Athens can be seen by comparing the geographical distribution of Greek literature over time. We know the names of a number of epic, lyric, and elegiac poets from the Archaic period, although most of their work is lost. These names are associated with various places: the islands of Paros and Thasos (Arkhilokhos), Keos (Simonides, Bakkhylides), and Lesbos (Sappho, Alkaios); the Ionian cities of Kolophon (Mimnermos, Xenophanes), and Teos (Anakreon); and the mainland communities not only of Athens (Solon) and Sparta (Alkman, Tyrtaios), but also of Megara (Theognis), Thebes (Pindar), and nearby Askra (Hesiod). Nobody knows whether Homer really existed, but his name is traditionally associated with various places in Ionia and the Aegean islands, most notably Khios and Smyrna. What is significant about this list is not the detail but the distribution: Athens in the Archaic period was one city among many, but not yet the cultural centre of the Greek world.

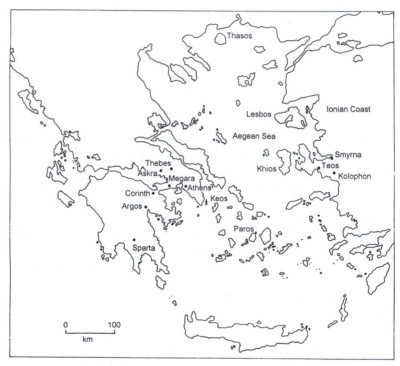

Fig. 2 Places Associated with Archaic Greek Writers. [Argos, Corinth and Thebes are included for comparison. The various writers associated with the places on this map are named in the text.]

The vast bulk of surviving Greek literature, however – or at any rate of the authors who form the traditional literary canon – dates from the Classical period, and almost all of it relates to Athens. Greek drama, for instance, is a characteristically Athenian phenomenon. It is not just that the genre seems to have originated there, and that the fifth-century tragic poets Aeschylus, Sophocles and Euripides, as well as the comedians Aristophanes and Menander, were all Athenian citizens. It is also that their surviving plays (with the notable exception of Euripides' *Bacchae*, written in self-imposed exile in Macedon) were composed for performance at Athenian civic/religious festivals, and served to explore what it was to be an Athenian. Much the same applies to other types of literature: Greek philosophy seems to have originated elsewhere, particularly in Ionia, but from the late fifth century onwards it was dominated either by Athenians like Plato (the first philosopher whose work survives), or else by visiting intellectuals based in Athens like Aristotle.

The writing of history is another fifth-century genre, and here the picture is slightly more complex. Herodotus, the inventor of history (writing perhaps in the 430s), came from Halikarnassos in Asia Minor, and seems to have travelled throughout the Greek world and beyond. The account of the Persian War which fills the latter part of his work is reasonably fair to all parties, but part at least of his aim is to explain the new phenomenon that is the rise of Athens (e.g. 5.66, 5.78); and he appears to accept what are presumably Athenian claims that their unique role in repelling the Persians gave them a right to subsequent leadership (7.139). His immediate successor Thucydides, on the other hand, was himself Athenian, but spent much of his adult life in exile (424-404 BC): despite Thucydides' claim that this gave him exceptional facilities for seeing contemporary events from both sides (5.26), he complains elsewhere that Spartan secretiveness made it impossible for him to discover as much about Sparta as he would have liked (e.g. 5.68). Both Herodotus and Thucydides are, in their different ways, Athenocentric historians.

Images and Counter-Images

Readers of ancient Greek history since antiquity have tended to focus on the Classical period, because that is when the mass of surviving canonical literature was produced: even today, one of the functions of history is to provide the background for the 'great books' in the literary canon. Readers of Classical history have tended to focus on Athens, since that is the society to which most of the surviving literature relates.

This is perhaps unavoidable, but it has important and dangerous consequences. It is all too easy for Athens (about which we know relatively much) to become our image of what a Greek *polis* should be like. Sparta, on the other hand, is a society about which even contemporary Greeks knew very little. Herodotus saw Sparta and Athens as co-operating rivals for the leadership of Greece (e.g. 1.56, cf. 1.59-68), but he regarded the Spartans as so odd that he gave them the sort of ethnographic treatment which otherwise he reserves for non-Greek peoples (6.56-60). Thucydides, as we have seen, found them impossibly secretive, but it is his treatment of the Peloponnesian

War (as we shall see in ch. 5) which identifies these two societies as rival claimants for the minds of his readers. If Athens is our ideal *polis*, then Sparta becomes an antitype: an alternative *polis*, onto which we ourselves (following the lead offered by non-Spartan Greeks) unload our images of what it is to be the opposite of an Athenian.

In reality, however, Sparta and Athens were two very unusual *poleis* among several hundred others. Both were exceptional in size and power and resources. Athens, for instance, seems to have had some 30,000 adult male citizens, a greater number than any other mainland *polis*: it was the availability of citizen manpower, as much as the wealth derived from their silver-mines at Laureion, which enabled the Athenians throughout most of the fifth century to control an empire of subject-allies. But the number of citizens was itself made possible by an unusually large sovereign territory, covering the whole of the peninsula of Attica (roughly 1,000 square miles or 2,400 square kilometres). At first sight, the relationship of Athens and Attica might seem to be paralleled by the position of Thebes within the plain of Boiotia, but there

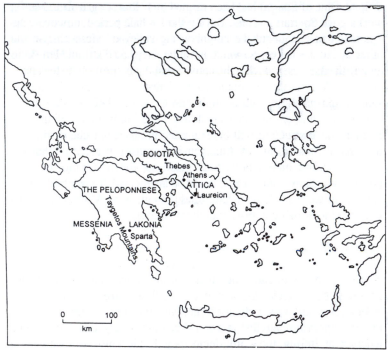

Fig. 3 Sparta and Athens in the Greek World. [The places named on this map are those mentioned in the text.]

is in fact a crucial difference. Thebes was only one of a number of *poleis* in Boiotia, and was continually struggling to maintain its position as the leader of a Boiotian confederacy; when Thebes was weak, it was because other Boiotian *poleis* had succeeded in disputing this leadership or breaking away. The whole of Attica, however, was the *polis* of Athens. The *sunoikismos* (unification) of Attica was the alleged achievement of the mythological hero Theseus, and this had happened so long ago that it would have been unthinkable for inhabitants of the villages of Attica (themselves Athenians) to campaign for independence from Athens.

The power of Sparta, on the other hand, depended not on the size of its citizen body (which seems never to have exceeded 10,000 adult males, and to have declined progressively and spectacularly over time), but on the way in which this was resourced. Unlike any other state in the Greek world, at least until the rise of Macedon in the fourth century, Sparta went in for direct imperialism. Since time immemorial, the Spartan homeland of Lakonia (the area surrounding Lakedaimon, the official name of Sparta) had been farmed by helots or agricultural serfs, working for Spartan masters. During the Archaic period, however, the Spartans had conquered the neighbouring valley of Messenia, on the other side of the Taygetos mountain-range; they had distributed the land among themselves, reducing the native inhabitants similarly to the status of helots. As a result, they could afford to restrict the status of Spartiate (full citizen) to those with enough land to devote their whole time to military training as absentee landlords. (The implications of this for Spartan social structure will be examined in ch. 3, and the distinctive patterns of Spartan and of Athenian imperialism in ch. 2.) What the Spartans lacked in numbers, they made up for by having the only professional army in Greece. It could be augmented at need by levying citizen militias from their subject-allies throughout the Peloponnese (the large peninsula that comprises southern Greece).

The Evils of Democracy

The most striking thing about Athens, however, was neither its size nor its power, but its social and, above all, its political structure. Athens was a democracy and we should not forget quite how disconcerting this was to contemporaries. We live in a world in which everybody claims to be a democrat. Indeed, the word 'democracy' has lost most of its meaning and serves merely to denote regimes of which the speaker broadly approves. (This is one reason why we find it so hard to cope with the idea of a democracy being imperialist.) In Classical Greece, however, democracy was an exceptional system, practised in Athens and some other *poleis* under Athenian influence. Direct democracy at Athens was, as we shall see in chapter 4, far more radical than any modern representative democracy. It was disliked and distrusted not only by other Greeks but also by the Athenian upper class. The fact that much of the surviving literature was produced by or for upper-class Athenians makes it very difficult for us to reconstruct a positive image of Athenian democracy.

Athens, therefore, was in the eyes of educated contemporaries (many of them Athenians) not so much a model to follow as a dreadful warning of the dangers of mob rule. Some at least of the most vocal critics would have preferred to live in a society like Sparta, in which power was restricted to those of wealth and good breeding. The obvious name for such a system was oligarchy (lit. 'the rule of the few') – or, to substitute a polite term, aristocracy ('the rule of the best'). However, would-be oligarchs were discredited by the brutality of the failed attempt to introduce an oligarchic regime at Athens in 411 and especially in 404/3 BC, whereas the notorious secretiveness of Spartan society allowed the imagination free rein to construct not simply an image but an idealised image of what it was to be the opposite of an Athenian. It is against this background that we find political theorists by the late fourth century expressing their reservations about democracy by asserting that the best type of constitution to have was a 'mixed' one – a mystic blend of the three standard constitutional forms, monarchy, oligarchy (or 'aristocracy') and democracy – and foisting this on Sparta. Aristotle (*Politics* 2.6 = 1265b35-42) reveals the chief problem with such theorising: that nobody could identify the alleged democratic features within the Spartan constitution. (A later example of a mixed constitution theory will be discussed in ch. 7.)

It is easy for us to forget the lingering power of such sentiments. Only within the last hundred years has democracy lost its stigma. As late as the end of the eighteenth century, it was not democratic Athens but republican Rome which attracted the attention of constitutional reformers. This can be seen in the constitution of the USA, which was written in 1787, and which looks back to Roman rather than Greek models (as witnessed for instance in the use of the Latin term 'Senate' to denote one of the Houses of Congress). Sparta, on the other hand, was so little-known that it could serve as the pattern for any existing and desirable system of social organisation, whether in Revolutionary France or in Nazi Germany.

At the end of the twentieth century, our images are very different. Athens (despite Athenian imperialism) is democratic and good; Sparta is evil and totalitarian. But once again it is image as much as reality that we are confronting, and it is the history of these images which forms the focus of this book.

Chapter 2
Imperial Geography

Constructing the Polis

In the course of his introduction, Thucydides remarks that the physical remains of ruined cities (he is talking about Agamemnon's Mycenae) do not necessarily match the realities of power:

> If Sparta were to be deserted, leaving only the temples and the foundations of buildings, I think that as time passes those who come after us would doubt whether its power had really matched its reputation. Yet the Spartans rule two-fifths of the Peloponnese, and lead not only the entire Peloponnese but also many allies outside it. However, since the city has not been organised as a single entity and does not contain rich temples or monuments, but consists of a group of villages, as used to be the custom in early Greece, it would look relatively insignificant – whereas if Athens were to suffer the same fate, then one would imagine, on the basis of what one saw, that the city had been twice as powerful as it actually is.
>
> (Thucydides, 1.10)

At first sight, this remarkably far-sighted judgment is borne out by a glance at a modern plan of ancient Sparta, though it must be admitted that our knowledge is incomplete. Far less archaeological work has been done at Sparta than at Athens, and many things may remain to be discovered or identified. The fact remains, however, that the map is fairly bare and many of the features on it are post-Classical at least in their present form. There seems, for instance, to have been a Late Archaic temple at the sanctuary of Artemis Orthia, but the existing temple is Hellenistic, and the theatre there is Roman (the significance of this complex of buildings is discussed in ch. 7). Still less Classical are the city walls, which were first erected under the Hellenistic tyrant Nabis (c. 200 BC). In Thucydides' time, and much later, the *polis* of Sparta was unwalled and consisted of five separate villages: one of which (Amyklai) was far enough from the other four (Kynosoura, Limnai, Mesoa and Pitana) for it to remain outside when the walls were eventually built.

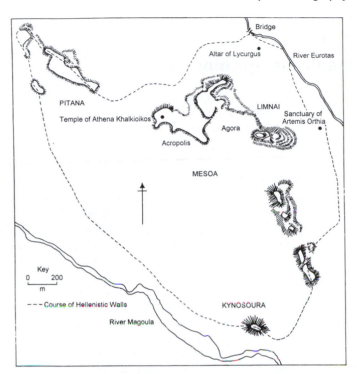

Fig. 4 Ancient Sparta. [Note the location of the villages (Amyklai is c. 5 miles south and off the map), the paucity of identified sites, and the course of the post-Classical walls].

Classical Sparta, then, was an ostentatiously non-ostentatious city. City-walls in antiquity were erected for two reasons: they offered protection, but they also served to demonstrate the wealth of a community that could afford to put them up. By not having walls, Sparta was publicly proclaiming its contempt for such displays of wealth. It was also claiming not to need artificial protection. When the Thebans invaded Lakonia after their decisive victory at Leuktra in 371 BC, it was the first time in over three hundred years that a foreign enemy under arms had crossed Spartan soil – hence the traditional Spartan claim that all their battles had been fought on enemy territory (see Plutarch, *Agesilaos* 31, for the same quip in two different versions). From this perspective, indeed, it was Sparta rather than Athens which matched the persuasive definition of the *polis* offered by the defeated Athenian general Nicias to his demoralised (and explicitly all-male) army cut off in Sicily in 413 BC: 'it is men who make a *polis*, not walls or ships with no men in them' (Thuc. 7.77).

Sparta: Conquest and Hegemony

In the passage quoted at the beginning of this chapter, Thucydides distinguishes between the Spartans 'ruling' (*nemontai*) two-fifths of the Peloponnese, and their 'leading' (*hêgountai*) the remainder. This reflects the distinction outlined in chapter 1 between sovereign or conquered territory (Lakonia and Messenia respectively, which together make up the southern two-fifths) and subject-allies (the rest).

The details of the Spartan conquest of Messenia are lost in the mists of Archaic pre-history. What purports to be a full account is given by the geographer Pausanias, writing in the second century AD, but the exploits of his alleged Messenian resistance heroes Aristomenes and Aristodemos are clearly fictitious, despite or perhaps because of the spurious precision with which he dates their respective deaths to 724 BC (Pausan. 4.13) and 668 BC (Pausan. 4.23). We cannot positively identify Pausanias' source here, and the only thing in his account for which there is good supporting evidence is that Messenia does indeed seem to have been conquered in two stages: there survive a few fragments of the mid-seventh-century war poet Tyrtaios, seeking to inspire his Spartan audience to resist an apparent rebellion (the so-called 'Second Messenian War') with stories of how their grandfathers had originally annexed Messenia. Perhaps the one thing that can be usefully inferred from Pausanias' narrative is that somebody in antiquity thought it worth forging a history of Messenian resistance – presumably after 369 BC, when Messene (as we shall see in ch. 6) was re-established by the Thebans as an independent *polis*. The difference between the helots (agricultural serfs) of Messenia and those of Lakonia was that the former retained an ancestral folk-memory of having been outside Spartan control.

The first surviving narrative account of Spartan imperialism is that of Herodotus (1.65-68), and it is striking that he has nothing to say here about Messenia. He concentrates instead on Sparta's treatment of Tegea, the southernmost city of the Arkadian plateau in the central Peloponnese, and hence the obvious next target for Spartan expansionism. Herodotus relates a fascinating story of how the Spartans, following a typically ambiguous oracle, had had their first attack defeated at the 'battle of the fetters' (so called because the Spartans had brought fetters to the battle with the evident intention of reducing the Tegeans to the same condition as the Messenians); following another oracle, a Spartan agent had discovered and brought home from Tegea a buried body purporting to be that of the hero Orestes, and the Spartans had consequently succeeded not in conquering the Tegeans, but in imposing an alliance on them. This became the pattern, and by c. 550 BC the Spartans had reduced most of the cities of the Peloponnese to the status of subject-allies.

We are left guessing how much of this story is true, and how far it simply represents the way in which fifth-century Spartans explained to Herodotus what does seem to have been a genuine change in policy. In Greek myth, the Heroic Age had been followed by the Dorian invasion of the Peloponnese. Spartans during the historical period could perceive themselves as descendants of invading Dorians, destined to rule by conquest. Sparta itself, however, had been an important Mycenaean site: it was the home of Helen (of Trojan War fame) and her deserted husband Menelaos, brother of Agamemnon the Achaean High King of Mycenae.

Orestes had been Agamemnon's son and heir. By appropriating his remains, the Spartans were claiming to be not simply Dorian conquerors (as in Lakonia and Messenia) but also the senior Achaean power within the Peloponnese, giving them the right of hegemony or leadership. The cities of the central and northern Peloponnese were gradually forced to acknowledge this claim, and what modern scholars term the 'Peloponnesian League' was a series of alliances by which individual cities bound themselves to follow Spartan leadership in war. At first sight, this new policy of hegemonial imperialism appears far more lenient than the earlier territorial conquest; and the allied cities had in theory the right of internal self-government. The alliances, however, were unequal, and although the allies seem to have had some collective voice in the form of a League Congress, it was the Spartans (as in Thuc. 1.66-88) who really decided policy.

Sparta portrayed itself as a conservative power, whose security was the product of harmony among Spartan citizens. Like most aspects of Sparta's self-image, these claims are only partly true. Sparta's primary sphere of influence was certainly the Peloponnese, and this seems to have been offered as a reason (or perhaps an excuse) for allowing the Athenians rather than themselves to lead the would-be alliance of island states against Persia from 478 BC that became the basis of Athenian imperialism. Nevertheless the Spartans were ready when it suited them to intervene outside the Peloponnese. Spartan leadership against the Persian invasion in 480-479 could be represented as pre-empting a threat to the Peloponnese itself; but in the final decade of the sixth century, Athens – which was clearly outside the Peloponnese – had been invaded three times and threatened on a fourth by Spartans (Herodotus 5.62-5, 5.70-3, 5.74-6, and cf. 5.90-2). The Spartan king Kleomenes, forbidden by the priestess on one of these occasions from entering a temple which was barred to Dorians, is said to have replied that he was 'an Achaean not a Dorian' (Herodotus 5.72), a quip which is revealing on two levels. In his eyes, the policy of Achaean leadership justifies intervention not just in the Peloponnese but throughout the Greek world. Moreover, this is a chance for Kleomenes to distinguish himself from his half-brother, whom he seems to have hated, and who bore the significant name Dorieus ('the/a Dorian'), a name which may indicate a policy difference underlying a family feud.

The Spartans were described by Thucydides as 'traditionally slow to go to war unless they were forced into it' (1.118). The context of this remark – which may itself be part of the Spartan myth – is Sparta's apparent unwillingness to resist Athenian expansion during the period 478-431 BC. But precisely what constitutes a vital national interest is a subjective judgment. Thucydides in his next sentence acknowledges that they were involved in wars at home during this period: these presumably included the great helot revolt of the 460s, and a chance remark by Herodotus (9.35) implies the existence between 478 and c. 465 of two major battles at Tegea and at Dipaieis against subject-allies apparently trying to secede from the Peloponnesian League.

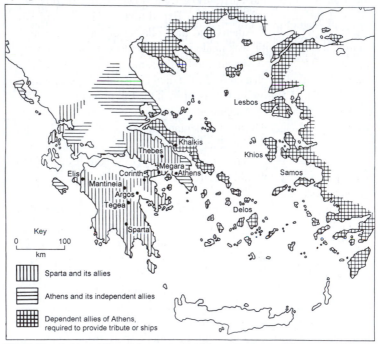

Fig. 5 The Subject-Allies of Sparta and of Athens in 431 BC. [The power of Sparta was based on the land, and that of Athens on its control of the sea.]

Athens: League and Empire

By the time of the Persian invasion of 480-479 BC, Sparta was already an established imperial power. Athenian imperialism, on the other hand, was a new phenomenon, which developed very rapidly in response to a perception of continuing Persian threat after 478. In that year the Athenians, who had supplied the bulk of the Greek fleet against the invading Persians, were invited to lead a would-be coalition of maritime *poleis*. The aims of those involved will have included the liberation of those cities still under Persian control, revenge for acts of destruction committed by the Persians in Greece, and mutual protection against any future threat. The precise balance between these aims is impossible for us now to determine, and may not have been clearly specified at the time.

The power of Athens, unlike that of Sparta, lay in its fleet. Whereas Sparta's subject-allies filled a land-mass (the Peloponnese), the geographical centre of Athenian imperial power was at all times the islands and above all the coastline of the Aegean Sea. This remained true from the successful liberation from Persia of the Ionian coast of Asia Minor in the 470s and early 460s, right down to the revolts which followed the defeat of the Sicilian Expedition in 413 BC and which ushered in the fall of Athens and the collapse of the empire in 404. Admittedly an attempt was made in the 450s to expand inland at the expense of Thebes and Megara (and at the same time abroad, by helping a native Egyptian revolt against the Persians), but these experiments were soon abandoned, following the collapse of the Egyptian revolt in 454 BC and the break-away of Megara and Thebes c. 447. At the same time, however, the financial basis of Athenian power was increasingly centred in Athens itself. In 454 the allied treasury was moved from the central Aegean island of Delos (a religious sanctuary) to Athens itself, evidently on the pretext that it would be safer there from any threat following the Egyptian disaster.

The style of Athenian imperialism was very different from that of Sparta. We have seen how the Spartans cultivated an image of archaising austerity (absence of city-walls, etc.), and how they demanded military service from their allies. Ships, on the other hand, were expensive to maintain and above all to replace if lost or damaged, and from the outset large numbers of the smaller maritime allies (many of which were little more than fishing villages) provided Athens with cash-contributions in lieu. There was moreover a gradual and (it seems) a largely voluntary shift, until by 440 the only ship-providers apart from Athens were Lesbos, Khios and Samos, the three largest island states. The system of cash-levies enabled the Athenians to flaunt their imperial control. Athens was at the outset a wealthy city and its imperial income gave it unparalleled wealth: the Greek word *phoros* (lit. 'contributions') gradually acquired connotations similar to those of the conventional translation 'tribute'.

Fig. 6 Fragments of the Athenian Tribute List for 440/39 BC. [The inset drawing shows the positions of the individual numbered fragments. The formulaic style of these texts helped make it possible to assemble them: in a given year, regions are named in large letters (including here 'Hellespont' and 'Around Thrace') and then follows a list of payments from individual cities.]

The establishment and development of Athenian imperial power is vastly better attested than that of Sparta, but the evidence creates its own problems. Some immediately contemporary material survives in the form of inscriptions carved on stone, and both the fact as well as the detail of this can be significant. The Athenians, as we saw, transferred the imperial treasury from Delos to Athens in 454 BC: in that year begins an annual sequence of texts known as the Athenian Tribute Lists (conventionally abbreviated to ATLs), although strictly speaking what they record is the one-sixtieth of each city's *phoros* which was given as a tithe to the goddess Athene, patron of the city of Athens and therefore of the alliance. The fact that the Athenians chose to display this information in such a public and permanent form is itself significant. So is the fact that laws and decrees, and records of public officials' expenditure, were also frequently inscribed, and progressively more so following the establishment of full democracy in the 460s.

The details of surviving inscriptions are often hard to interpret. Rarely do stones survive intact, or even in sufficient fragments to restore the whole. The sequence of ATLs, for instance, has been established with considerable probability, but even so it is sometimes unclear which fragment belongs to which year in the sequence. Nor does the text provide its own context: we may be able to see that a particular ally paid more or less than usual in a given year, or to infer that it paid late or paid nothing, but without independent evidence we cannot tell why. This lack of context is a particular problem with one of the most interesting types of inscription, those recording decisions taken by the assembly. Such decrees do not form sequences, and before 410 BC they do not normally record their year. For example, we have a decree imposing terms on the defeated city of Khalkis in Euboia, which is conventionally dated c. 447 BC, but the evidence for this date is that it provides a context for a revolt of the island. Similarly, the decree imposing on all allies the use of Athenian weights, measures and coinage can only be dated on the basis of letter-forms and of general probabilities. It is alarming that scholars' estimates vary from the 440s to the 420s, because these different dates allow for very different reconstructions of the developing tone of Athenian imperialism.

To set such disparate fragments of information in a coherent context we need a narrative history, and the obvious place to turn is Thucydides. Thucydides' history of the Peloponnesian War begins in 431 BC. All he offers us before this is a brief narrative summary of the *pentêkontaëtia* or 'fifty-year period' (1.89-117, actually covering 478-435 BC), which fills some sixteen pages in modern translations. For reasons that we shall discover, this is hardly the basis for a satisfactory framework, but it is the best we have. There is what purports to be a rival account by Diodoros, writing in the first century BC, but on examination this seems to be simply a garbled reworking of Thucydides, perhaps at second remove. We do possess a monograph from the 320s, written either by Aristotle or by a pupil, on the Athenian Constitution (*Athêniaôn Politeia*, hereafter *Ath.Pol.*), which incorporates a chrono-logical survey of constitutional development to 403 BC. The section covering our period (§§23-28) is derivative and disappointing, though it does preserve traces of non-Thucydidean interpretations of Athenian imperialism. Also worth mentioning is the biographer Plutarch (c. 100 AD), several of whose *Lives* are of people active during our period. Plutarch was a voracious reader, and although he offers no chronological framework he does preserve interesting anecdotes, some of which may go back to reliable sources. However, Plutarch was writing five hundred years after the events and he does not have a sympathetic understanding of democratic Athens. As we shall see, it is often difficult to determine what lies behind particular details.

Thucydides' *pentêkontaëtia* excursus is a very odd text. The events mentioned are carefully placed in order, but no dates are given, and few indications of time. Chronologies can be constructed on this basis, but they are relative rather than absolute, and there is lingering dispute between rival scholarly schemes. More significant is the fact that Thucydides is deliberately selective. His aim is to illustrate the growth of Athenian power, so nothing is said about possible Spartan difficulties with its Peloponnesian League allies (above). Even on Thucydides' own terms, there are odd gaps, with no mention for instance of the Athenians founding the important colony of Amphipolis on the North Aegean coast. One apparent omission demands special notice: despite Thucydides' silence, it is generally believed that c. 449 BC the Athenians forced Persia formally to concede the independence of the Greek cities of Ionia (now tributary to Athens). If so, this is an astonishing silence – though there is at least the possibility that Thucydides is right, and that the so-called 'Peace of Kallias' was invented by fourth-century Athenian propagan-dists eager to reconstruct a heroic past.

We should beware of Thucydides' success, here as elsewhere, in imposing his viewpoint on us. Thucydides believes that Athens hijacked an alliance of willing volunteers and gradually turned it into an empire, and he engages in at least some special pleading. If protection was one of the functions of the alliance, then the Athenians had at least a defensible case in suppressing the revolt of Naxos, the first of the allies to seek to opt out. Thucydides (1.98), however, describes Athens' action as 'enslavement' (which seems extreme) and 'unprecedented' (without stopping to compare Spartan behaviour in similar situations). The dominance of Thucydides' view of Athenian imperialism can be seen in the language which has conditioned modern scholarship on the subject. Textbooks conventionally speak of the (nice) 'Delian League' being transformed from 454 onwards into the (nasty) 'Athenian Empire'.

This is a possible interpretation, but not the only one possible. The *Ath.Pol.*, for instance, speaks of the Athenians 'deciding to treat their [cash-contributing] allies in a more masterful fashion' (*Ath.Pol.* 24.2), in a context which seems to refer to the 470s. That implies a view that Athens was blatantly imperialistic almost from the start. Moreover, the distinction between 'League' and 'Empire' has no basis in ancient linguistic usage. Speakers in Thucydides speak informally of the Athenian *'arkhê'* ('rule', abstract noun), and inscriptions occasionally mention 'places which the Athenians rule', but there is no clear shift from gentler to more severe language, and formal terminology (for what that is worth) remained at all times 'the Athenians and their allies'.

Our sources imply that Athens was unpopular among its allies in a way that Sparta was not (or at least not before 404). Certainly Spartan propaganda in 431 was that they were fighting 'to free the Greeks [i.e. from slavery to Athens]' (Thuc. 2.8). On one level, the relative unpopularity of Athens may be because Sparta (like Rome) supported traditional ruling classes in its allied cities, and these were the people who made their views known. Hints survive in our texts of various features of Athenian imperialism which may have irritated particularly the ruling class among the allies. Aristophanes in the *Birds* parodies the sending of Athenian officials to keep an eye on allied cities. The decree imposing terms on Khalkis (above) insists on important legal cases being transferred to Athenian jurisdiction. The same point is applied more generally in an early and intriguing anti-democratic pamphlet mis-attributed in antiquity to Xenophon and so known confusingly either as the 'Old Oligarch' or as '[Xen.] (i.e., pseudo-Xenophon) *Ath.Pol.*':

> The Athenian *dêmos* [common people] benefits from the fact that trials for the allies are held at Athens.... Because of this, the allies have become even more the slaves of the Athenian *dêmos*.
>
> ([Xen.], *Ath.Pol.*, 1.18)

Above all, perhaps, it was a question of money and style. Plutarch (*Pericles* 12) reports a debate over the legitimacy of using surplus allied

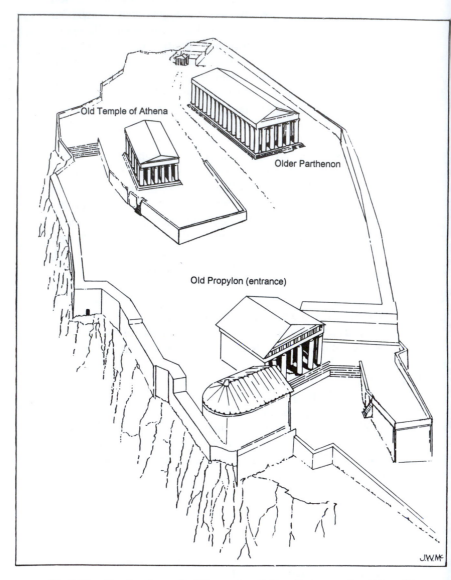

Fig. 7 The Athenian Acropolis: (this page) c. 500 BC, (facing page) c. 400 BC. [The monumentalisation of power under Pericles can be seen in the increased number of buildings, and particularly in the reorientation of the entrance: in 500 this had been angled, to provide defence; by 400, it had been made to face straight forwards, so as to impress the viewer.]

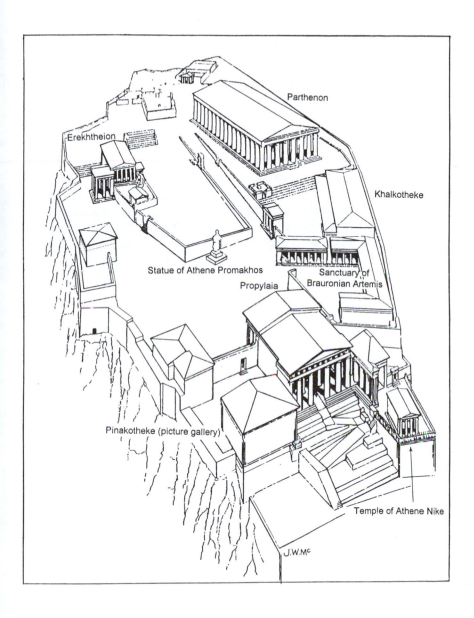

Parthenon

Erekhtheion

Khalkotheke

Statue of Athene Promakhos

Sanctuary of
Brauronian Artemis

Propylaia

Pinakotheke (picture gallery)

Temple of Athene Nike

J.W.Mc

tribute to fund a programme of public buildings on the Athenian Acropolis. Whether such a debate (and particularly the alleged arguments against) could ever have taken place in the Athenian assembly has been seriously questioned, and the whole story may be a fiction. The fact remains, however, that it was by means of surplus tribute that the buildings were funded (Parthenon 447-438 BC, Propylaia 437-432, Temple of Athene Nike 427-424). There are, following some reconstructions, 192 male figures in the procession on the frieze of the Parthenon, precisely the number of Athenians killed at Marathon in 490: this may be a claim to primacy, on the grounds of having been the first Greeks to defeat Persia. Putting up impressive buildings was something often done by tyrants, like the Peisistratids in sixth-century Athens. There had been some reconstruction after the Persian sack of the Acropolis in 480, but the Periclean building programme changed the face of the most visible feature of the city. It could be interpreted as the Athenian *dêmos* representing itself as the tyrant, and the allies as its subjects.

Chapter 3

Democracy, Oligarchy, and the Distribution of Power

Minority Rule in Democratic Athens

Athens and Sparta shared a system of minority rule by male citizens. There were substantial differences both in the distribution of power among citizens, and in the relationship between citizens and the rest of the population. But Athenian democracy is a system as alien to us as is oligarchy at Sparta.

The term 'democracy' (*dêmokratia*) is found in Athenian sources from the mid-fifth century. In this chapter, it will be used to describe what is often called 'full' or 'radical' democracy, the system created by the reforms of Ephialtes in the 460s; and we shall concentrate on the democratic system as it operated from Ephialtes until its abolition in 322 following the Macedonian conquest. Earlier reformers, like Solon (c. 590) and Cleisthenes (c. 510), are often regarded as democrats or proto-democrats. However, they do not appear to have used the term, and we should beware of assuming that they saw themselves as preparing the way for Ephialtes. Their achievements will be considered briefly in the final section of this chapter.

Dêmokratia means 'the power of the *dêmos*'. *Dêmos* can denote either 'the people of Athens' or 'the common people', but it did not include non-Athenians, and Athenian male citizens comprised a relatively small proportion of the population. No statistics survive from antiquity; modern estimates are in the range of 30-60,000 citizens immediately before the Peloponnesian War, dropping in the fourth century to some 20-30,000 as a result of losses both of manpower and of imperial wealth. These figures are for adult males only. Whether Athenian women can be classified as 'citizens' is itself debatable, since they possessed neither the vote nor any other active citizen rights – though women did play important religious roles (as priestesses, etc.), and as we shall see, the civic status of an Athenian mother became important after 450.

What made you a citizen was not where you lived or where you were born, but your parentage. Originally you had simply to have a citizen father, but a law proposed by Pericles in 451/0 and reaffirmed in 403/2 restricted citizenship to those born of citizen parents on both sides. Any free non-Athenian, whether Greek or foreign, was entitled to live in Athens as a metic (Gk. *metoikos*). There seem to have been some 10,000 adult male metics (plus women and children) at the start of the Peloponnesian War. A few will have been extremely rich, and socially superior to the mass of poor citizens, but metics resided on sufferance and without political rights.

Slaves on the other hand were chattels, the property of their owners, with neither active nor passive rights. Ideally – though perhaps not always in practice – they were non-Greeks. Numbers cannot be determined. Occasional ancient estimates in the hundreds of thousands may simply reflect an impression that slaves outnumbered free in wealthy households (though probably not overall).

We today are conditioned to assume that democracy is about the abolition of privilege. This leads to the assumption, conveniently ignoring the American example, that democracy and imperialism cannot go together. Athenian democracy exploited slaves at home and (whenever possible) subject-allies abroad. The blatant exploitation of slaves – and possibly also of women – made it appear that citizens were not exploited and that they had equal access to privilege. The effect, and possibly one of the aims, of Pericles' citizenship law was to preserve the privileged status of citizen by restricting access to it. We should beware of complaining that such a society does not deserve to be called democracy: partly because the ancient users of a Greek word have as much right to interpret its meaning as we do, but also because Athenian democracy offered ordinary citizens unique access to decision-making.

Athens was a direct democracy, wholly unlike modern representative systems. In the fifth century, all decisions were taken in the assembly (*ekklêsia*), which met every nine days or so, and at which every citizen over 18 could attend, speak and vote. Assembly decisions might be challenged in the lawcourts, but this did not reduce popular control of power, because the *dikastai* (jurors-cum-judges) were a non-professional cross-section of citizens over 30 (which was apparently the normal minimum age for public office at Athens). There was no parliament. Indeed there was no government, in the sense of a group responsible for developing coherent public policies. There were no political parties of the type with which we are familiar. Political alliances were unstable, because without party manifesto and party whip, political leaders could not guarantee to deliver votes.

The democratic council (*boulê*) of 500 members served as the assembly's standing committee, coping with emergencies and preparing the agenda, but inscriptions show that the assembly often amended its proposals. Councillors served a one-year rotating term: you could serve only twice, and not in consecutive years. This prevented the undoubted power of the council being monopolised by a few powerful individuals. Councillors were not elected but appointed by lot, to give everyone a fairer chance. Indeed, election to office was regarded by Greek political theorists as characteristic of oligarchy rather than of democracy, on the ground that elections favour those who are well known.

One of the tasks of the council was to supervise the public officials (*arkhai*). There were large numbers of these, but their tasks were normally to carry out the assembly's decisions rather than to initiate policy. The vast majority of public officials were appointed by lot for a one-year term without the possibility of re-appointment. The ten generals (*stratêgoi*), however, were elected and could be re-elected. This was a post which allowed some scope for individual competence, and the fact that a general was elected gave him some political authority. In the fifth century, the generalship was held for long periods by political leaders like Pericles (443-429); but even Pericles, like any other holder of public office, always remained accountable in court for his actions, and in 429 was deposed and heavily fined.

The ordinary Athenian had access in theory to considerable power, but the practice is harder to determine. Evidence for political participation comes mainly from the fourth century, when the assembly seems regularly to have achieved the quorum of 6,000 needed for certain types of business. In one fifth-century source (Thuc. 8.72), the oligarchic revolutionaries of 411 BC claim that meetings during the War have never attracted even 5,000. It would suit the oligarchs to exaggerate the problem, but possibly the situation improved when pay was introduced, some time after 403/2, for those attending.

The figure of 6,000 may sound small, but if for example 2,000 attended each meeting, 2,000 alternate meetings, and 2,000 one meeting in four, then the total attending at least ten of forty meetings annually would be 14,000 (1 x 2,000 + 2 x 2,000 + 4 x 2,000). What such conjectures represent as a proportion of the citizen body depends of course on total citizen numbers. This problem applies even more to calculations based on council membership. Of the positions appointed by lot, this was the only one that could be held twice in a lifetime, which implies that there would have been problems finding 500 new councillors annually, but not 250. Modern estimates of citizen numbers, however, rest partly on assumptions about how many citizens would take on such an onerous task.

Political activity can occur at several levels. An ordinary citizen might attend the assembly or sit in the lawcourts with some regularity, or even serve on the council. Political leaders, who proposed motions or held high office or prosecuted each other, were rich men. Admittedly, comic dramatists portray the so-called demagogues of the late fifth century as gutter politicians. Kleon, for instance, is caricatured as a tanner, and Hyperbolos and Kleophon as sellers of lamps and of lyres respectively. But we should be wary of inferring that these were factory workers, or even self-made men.

Fig. 8 *Ostrakon* of Kleophon, c. 416 BC. [The text (scratched in a rather good script) reads 'Kleophon the son of Kleippides of [A]charnae'. (Acharnae was his deme or parish, for which see the final section of this chapter.)]

Fig. 8 shows a ballot prepared for an ostracism, probably in 416 BC. Ostracism was an odd institution, virtually obsolete by this date, in which votes were cast to exile an individual by naming him on an *ostrakon* (a fragment of pottery, in this case a roof-tile). The discovery of this *ostrakon* in 1968 made clear what was not previously known: that Kleophon was the son of Kleippides, who served as general in 429/8. The Athenian generalship had a property qualification – which shows that Kleophon had at least one generation of wealth behind him.

It is significant that ostracism was a vote against an individual rather than for a party. We should not pretend that democracy enabled poor Athenians to be political leaders, but the absence of political parties increased individual competition for political prizes; and this enabled the *dêmos* to distribute political success and failure by its votes in the assembly and the courts.

Spurious Equality at Sparta

Spartiates (full Spartan citizens) were known as *homoioi*, which roughly means 'equals' (lit. 'those who are similar'). This piece of persuasive rhetoric (one wonders who it was aimed at) is clearly untrue: Herodotus (7.134) describes two individuals as 'in birth and wealth among the foremost'. There was however a point behind it. All Spartiates had been through the same educational system, the *agôgê* (on which see ch. 4), and an important function of shared upbringing is to instill collective values. The Spartan *agôgê* was a military education and among its prime values were conformity and obedience.

This has obvious political implications. Sparta, like Athens, had a citizen assembly (probably called the *ekklêsia*, as at Athens, though earlier scholars often refer to it as the *apella*). But the Spartan assembly was a meeting of soldiers, and habits of obedience do not encourage criticism. Moreover, whereas Athenian assembly meetings opened with the invitation 'who wishes to speak?', at Sparta the presiding official seems to have chosen the speakers; and we see no equivalent of the Athenian assembly's right to propose amendments. Thucydides (1.79-87) describes the Spartan assembly deciding in 432 BC to declare war on Athens: a long speech against war is made by King Arkhidamos, followed by a blunt and short speech by the ephor Sthenelaidas, the presiding official. Certainly the assembly had a real choice to make here, but the public disagreement between two such prominent individuals suggests that those in the inner circle of power were unusually divided, and the assembly was being called upon to arbitrate rather than simply to ratify.

Many *poleis* claimed to have abolished kingship in the remote past. Sparta, a self-consciously archaising state, had not one king but two, from separate royal families (Eurypontids and Agiads, on which see fig. 9 below). For other Spartans, status was something to be achieved; for kings, it was ascribed. Herodotus (6.56-9) lists their ceremonial rights (extra food, elaborate funeral, etc.), important in a world where visible prestige is power. He highlights religious privileges, including control over oracles, and he alludes to their right of military command. In fact a full Spartan army could be commanded only by a king or his regent, which led Aristotle to describe the kings as hereditary generals (*Politics* 3.14 = 1285a7). Plutarch says that the heir apparent of a Spartan king was the only person exempted from the *agôgê* (*Agesilaos* 1), and we may speculate on possible reasons. It would be disastrous for him to perform badly in a highly competitive environment (though correspondingly he lost the chance of performing outstandingly well). But his exemption also symbolised the explicit inequality of a future king, as the one person who was not expected to grow up obeying orders.

Whereas kingship was hereditary, the five ephors were elected for a one-year term. Xenophon says that ephors and kings exchanged oaths every month, and it is striking that he identifies the ephors so closely with the city that he uses the latter term for the former:

> The ephors swear on behalf of the city, the king for himself. The king swears that he will rule according to the established laws of the city, the city [not 'the ephors'] to do no damage to the royal authority provided the king keeps his oath.
>
> (Xenophon, *Lak.Pol.*, 15.7)

There is also a studied inequality in the oaths, in that only the ephors are allowed a let-out clause. The ephors could legally arrest a king (Thuc. 1.131), and had unrestricted jurisdiction over other officials (Xen. *Lak.Pol.* 8.4); indeed, the fact that *ephoraô* means 'to oversee' implies a right to keep an eye on everything. Admittedly Aristotle (*Politics* 2.9 = 1270b10-12), writing c. 330 BC, complains that in his day the office was held by men who were 'poor and easily bribed', but declining Spartan power since 371 may have made the office less worth fighting for. On the other hand, theoretically powerful offices are not always held by people prepared to use their powers. The crucial thing may be that the ephor became a private citizen at the end of his year of office: making powerful enemies under such circumstances was risky, unless you were sure of winning.

The 28 members of the *gerousia* ('council of old men') were elected for life and had no such worries. The *gerousia* is sometimes portrayed in our sources as planning policy in advance, but this may be a confusion with the council at Athens (which did have that function). The best attested case is in 403 BC, when it is a majority of the ephors that King Pausanias had had to persuade (Xen. *Hell.* 2.4.29) before overturning Lysander's policy towards the Thirty at Athens; on his return, he was narrowly acquitted by a court comprising *gerousia*, ephors, and his fellow-king (Pausan. 3.5.2). A permanent criminal court, with the right to examine policy after the event, is a powerful political body. However, the *gerousia* is said to have had a minimum age of 60 (Plut. *Lycurgus* 26). Sparta was a society which respected old age, but the danger of senility was noted by Aristotle (*Politics* 2.9 = 1270b41); and the longer a king remained in office, the more members of the *gerousia* would have known and respected him as king while they were still private citizens.

Spartan kingship was a dangerous eminence: no fewer than six kings or regents seem to have been tried or deposed during the fifth century. But the long and powerful reigns of Kleomenes (c. 520-c. 490) and Agesilaos (c. 400-360) show what could be achieved by a king who was militarily successful, or good at patronage, or both. The career of Agesilaos, incidentally, rules out any theory of declining royal power.

Spartiates prided themselves on an image of internal harmony. Only rarely can we see enough to cast doubt on this – an episode of revolutionary plotting is revealed by Plutarch (*Agesilaos* 26) – but certainly there was no harmony in relations between Spartiates and helots. Helots were agricultural serfs allocated to the estates of Spartan citizens in Lakonia and Messenia, though the latter (for reasons discussed in ch. 2) were always more ready to revolt. The difference between Spartan helots and Athenian chattel slaves is partly that the latter were owned by individuals whereas the former were communally and collectively controlled by the Spartan state, which alone could free them. More significantly, the helots lived in their own communities and were themselves Greeks.

The mass enslavement of a native population has some parallels in other deeply traditional Greek communities (our sources mention the so-called *penestai* in Thessaly, and the *klarôtai* in Crete). What was unique was not the Spartan exploitation of such labour-power but its systematic repression. Plutarch claims that each year the ephors declared war on the helots, so that to kill them would not incur religious pollution (*Lycurgus* 28). A massacre of 2,000 helots is reported by Thucydides (4.80), who claims that the manner of their death had remained characteristically secret. He adds in a notoriously ambiguous aside that 'Spartan policy with reference to the helots has always been based almost entirely on the idea of security', or alternatively that 'Spartan policy has always been based on security with reference to the helots'.

Other subject groups existed within the Spartan state. We know little about the *perioikoi* (lit. 'those who live round about'), except that they lived in villages mainly in Lakonia, and were apparently free non-Spartans with limited rights of internal self-government. In addition, there were various categories of sub-citizen Spartans. We hear of restrictions on those who retreated or surrendered in battle (the *tresantes* or 'tremblers', Plut. *Agesilaos* 30). The *hupomeiones* or 'inferiors', on the other hand, seem to be those who became too poor to pay the contribution to their *sussition* (military dining-club) which qualified them for citizenship – a significant group, given Aristotle's belief that a progressive concentration of land in fewer hands had caused the catastrophic fall in Spartiate manpower (for which see ch. 6). It was presumably this manpower shortage which led to selected helots being freed by the Spartan state to fight as *neodamôdeis* (first attested in the 420s). It is about this time that we hear also of *mothakes*, who seem to be the sons of poor citizens being sponsored through the *agôgê* by rich patrons: this may be an innovation designed specifically to remedy the shortage of Spartiates.

What made the helots dangerous was the declining number of Spartiates available to control them. The Spartan nightmare was that instead of acquiescing in Spartan rule, these other subordinate status-groups might decide to cast in their lot with the helots. Xenophon's account (*Hell.* 3.3.4-11) of the abortive conspiracy of Kinadon (c. 400 BC) reveals one occasion on which they seemed on the verge of doing this.

Charter-Myths and Ancient Lawgivers

A notable similarity between Athens and Sparta is that both societies perceived their own political system as the work of an ancient lawgiver.

Herodotus, writing c. 430, was told that Sparta had previously been politically unstable. In many *poleis*, such a situation had allowed power to be seized by a tyrant (not necessarily a bad man, but a non-constitutional ruler). At Sparta, according to Herodotus, the lawgiver Lycurgus had instead established *eunomia* (an untranslatable word with connotations of 'political stability' and 'good order'). He had first instituted a new and unchangeable body of laws, then reformed the army, and finally created the ephorate and the *gerousia*. How much of this story (1.65-6) Herodotus himself believes is uncertain. He reports the Delphic oracle as uncertain whether Lycurgus was a man or a god, which may hint at scepticism. However, he does in passing identify Lycurgus as regent for King Leobotas, traditionally dated c. 975 BC (although he also locates the achievement of *eunomia* shortly before the reigns of Leon and Agasikles, c. 600).

Thucydides' version (1.18) ignores Lycurgus, but states that *eunomia* had been established over 400 years before the end of the Peloponnesian War (i.e., c. 825-805). He heightens the contrast between Sparta and tyranny to the extent of claiming that Sparta had suppressed tyrannies throughout Greece: evidently this is yet another myth about Sparta, because it is hard to reconcile with Sparta's readiness to restore the tyrant Hippias at Athens c. 510 (Herodotus 5.91).

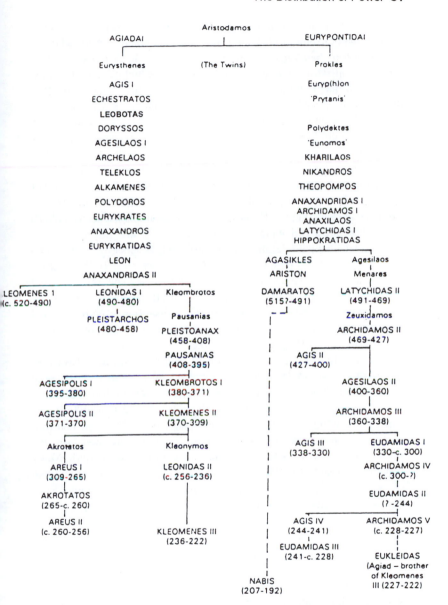

Fig. 9 The Agiad and Eurypontid Kings of Sparta. [The succession in each family becomes complex at precisely the point where we begin to know something about it. This suggests that the names in the earlier parts of the list reflect a historical legend.]

Plutarch, writing c. 100 AD, acknowledges in despair that earlier authors could not agree a date (*Lycurgus* 1). He himself prefers to make him regent for King Kharilaos (§3), traditionally dated c. 880. He does however quote an apparently genuine and very early constitutional document, the so-called Great Rhetra (§6: *rhêtra* is a Spartan word for 'law'). Its interpretation is almost as obscure to us as it was to Plutarch, but it gives pride of place to kings and *gerousia*, entirely omitting the ephors. The ephors are similarly absent from the fragments of the seventh-century poet Tyrtaios, whose significantly-titled poem *Eunomia* again praises *gerousia* and kings only. Plutarch himself reports a tradition that the ephorate was introduced 130 years later under King Theopompos (traditionally dated c. 750). For Herodotus the constitution of Lycurgus was a historical monolith, but the earlier sources reported by Plutarch suggest that the system had really been established by a series of piecemeal changes.

At Athens, on the other hand, Solon does seem to have existed and his activity can be dated c. 590 (or possibly c. 570). We possess fragments of his poems, quoted in *Ath.Pol.*'s account (§§5-12) and throughout Plutarch's *Life of Solon*. However, the fragments are mostly short, and consist largely of moralising generalisations. Specific political details have to be extracted not from the fragments themselves but from glosses offered by Plutarch and *Ath.Pol.*

The traditional interpretation of Solon is that his activity as lawgiver took place against a background of economic crisis, with poor farmers having become *hektêmoroi* (lit. 'sixth-part people'), in debt to their richer neighbours and obliged to surrender a proportion of their produce to them, with the risk of being enslaved if they defaulted. Solon abolished hektemorage by banning 'debts on the security of the person' (i.e., those in which defaulters could be enslaved). Many modern scholars, however, prefer to see hektemorage as a traditional obligation to pay dues to a social superior. If so, then the motive force behind Solon becomes not an economic crisis but a gradual shift in social perceptions, and a developing sense that this is an improper way to treat members of the community. Its consequence, paradoxically, may have been the spread of chattel slavery, as landowners looked for alternatives to exploit.

Herodotus (1.29-34), our earliest source for Solon, claims to know very little about him. A few years after Herodotus, during the revolution of the Four Hundred (411 BC), both the oligarchic revolutionaries and their opponents claimed the ancestral constitution as authority for their proposals. An ideological propaganda-war ensued over what Solon had really been up to, with the result that anything said about Solon after this date (which includes *Ath.Pol.* and Plutarch) is likely to reflect fifth- and fourth-century perceptions rather than sixth-century reality.

Surviving sources say less about Cleisthenes (c. 510 BC), though his name too was invoked in 411 (*Ath.Pol.* 29.3). He established the democratic council and gave constitutional status to the demes (villages or civil parishes), each of which supplied a quota of councillors in proportion to its size. Deme-membership was hereditary and became the necessary qualification for citizenship – which was, in a sense, Cleisthenes' invention. Modern interpretations of his work rely on fourth-century inscriptions listing councillors and their demes, but it has recently been suggested that the quotas may have been revised at the democratic restoration in 403/2. If correct, this undermines attempts to use the fourth-century quota-system to answer the question, did Cleisthenes gerrymander the deme-map to his own political advantage?

Stories about lawgivers were told not because they were true, but as charter-myths to justify existing situations. All Athenians could appeal to Solon (more easily perhaps than to Cleisthenes). Like Lycurgus at Sparta, he was an idealisation of what Athens was about; we shall be looking in chapter 4 at other ways in which this image could be constructed.

Chapter 4
Life, Death, and the Organisation of Society

Becoming a Spartan

Education at Sparta was controlled by the state. We know of no other *polis* where that was the case; and it may have been unique, to judge from the praise which ancient political theorists lavished on Sparta for taking education seriously (e.g. Aristotle *Politics* 8.1 = 1337a31, though he had reservations about the curriculum). The Spartan *agôgê* (lit. 'upbringing') is given a central role in the alleged Lycurgan system by both Xenophon (*Lak.Pol.* 2-4) and Plutarch (*Lycurgus* 14-18).

The formal education of a Spartan boy began, according to Plutarch (*Lycurgus* 16), at the age of 7, though in another sense both he and Xenophon regard it as starting at or before birth. Both of them remark on the unusual fact that Spartan girls as well as boys undertook formal athletic training, and both consider that the purpose was to make them more likely to bear healthy children: a point which Xenophon (*Lak.Pol.* 1.3-4) associates closely with their sons' education, and which Plutarch (*Lycurgus* 14) regards as integral to it. Unsupported statements by Plutarch should be treated with caution as testimony for Classical practice, though they are good evidence at least for the development of Sparta's image by AD 100, and he particularly highlights the role of the state in questions of childbearing. Whereas an Athenian father was free to decide whether to rear or to expose his newborn children, Plutarch claims that at Sparta this decision was based on the baby's physical fitness and made by the tribal elders (*Lycurgus* 16).

Plutarch's picture of Spartan formal education is that of a boarding school or military camp, with boys taken away from their families and living in communal barracks (*Lycurgus* 16). Xenophon reinforces the impression of state-control when he contrasts Sparta with other cities:

> Instead of each citizen individually choosing slaves to be *paidagôgoi* [i.e., to look after boys outside school hours], Lycurgus placed in charge of them collectively one of those men who fill the great offices of state.
>
> (Xenophon, *Lak.Pol.*, 2.2)

Spartan boys seem to have been organised into age-classes, with older boys taking some responsibility for younger ones (Plutarch *Lycurgus* 17). Presumably such collective and continual supervision will have heightened competitiveness between those involved (cf. Xen. *Lak.Pol.* 4.3-6). Spartan education was designed to produce winners, and although we do not hear of people failing to complete the *agôgê*, the production of realistic winners necessarily implies losers.

The curriculum was essentially military. Archaic Sparta appears to have had a wide literary and artistic tradition: admittedly what survives of Tyrtaios' elegies (c. 650 BC) is narrowly militaristic, but the fragments of Alkman's choral lyrics (c. 630) include what may have been a wedding hymn, which could easily have come from any other major *polis* of the period. Lakonian pot-painting similarly seems to have flourished down to the second half of the sixth century. Classical Sparta professed to despise high culture, though Xenophon hints that choral singing still formed part of the curriculum (*Lak.Pol.* 4.2), and a story in Plutarch may imply that Alkman's poems were still approved in the fourth century BC (or that they

Fig. 10 Archaic Lakonian Cup showing Symposium Scene, c. 560 BC. [Aristocratic culture throughout Archaic Greece was based around the symposium (ritualised drinking party). The presence of a symposium scene on this drinking cup, and the quality of the workmanship, suggest that Archaic Sparta was more part of mainstream Greek culture than it later became.]

were not approved, *Lycurgus* 28). Several military anecdotes involving written messages imply the teaching of basic literacy, though the 'Lakonic' verbal skills on which Spartans prided themselves were primarily oral. Brevity, and the demolition of intellectual pretensions, were prized: the speech which Thucydides gives to Sthenelaidas in 432 BC (for which see ch. 3) is a highly self-conscious example of such rhetoric.

The *agôgê* leaves in our sources an impression of physical toughness. Aristotle indeed complained that it was over-physical, with emphasis on the single virtue of bravery to the neglect of others (*Politics* 8.4 = 1338b11-14). Xenophon emphasises harsh physical punishment (*Lak.Pol.* 2.2, 2.8, 2.9), and sparse allowances of food (*Lak.Pol.* 2.5) and clothing (barefoot, and only one garment permitted even in the coldest weather, *Lak.Pol.* 2.3-4). Plutarch characteristically adds picturesque details about stuffing mattresses with reeds which they had had to pick with their bare hands (*Lycurgus* 16).

Both Xenophon (*Lak.Pol.* 2.6-7) and Plutarch (*Lycurgus* 17) insist that the boys were expected to supplement their meagre rations by stealing; this was, according to Xenophon, a form of military training, and those who got caught were punished – not for dishonesty but for incompetence. Such training in guerilla tactics seems odd, if the aim was to produce hoplites or heavy infantry (for which see ch. 5). Indeed, this may be evidence that the need for covert operations against the helots had done more to undermine the hoplite ideal of formation fighting than the Spartans would admit. While on the subject of stealing, Plutarch adds the curious story of the Spartan boy who was apprehended with a fox-cub concealed in his clothing, and who allowed it fatally to disembowel him rather than owning up (*Lycurgus* 18). At first sight, this is simply an improving story about Spartan toughness (though with a moral point that might have shocked the young George Washington). The need to hide the fox, however, implies that it had a previous owner, and the desire to transport it alive implies that it is not to be used for food. One wonders precisely what is going on here.

A traditional part of the image of British boarding-school life is homosexuality. Given that a relationship between a young man and a teenage boy would have been regarded among Greek aristocrats as a normal part of the process of growing up, Xenophon treats this subject with remarkable defensiveness (*Lak.Pol.* 2.12-14): the aim, he insists, was to encourage hero-worship, not sex. The particular importance of such relationships at Sparta, however, may perhaps be seen in their continuing power to create networks of political patronage. Xenophon elsewhere recounts the illuminating story of how King Agesilaos was induced to vote for acquittal at the trial of Sphodrias (Spartan governor of Thespiai in 378 and patently guilty of illegal and diplomatically inept aggression against Athens), because Agesilaos' son Arkhidamos was the lover of Sphodrias' son Kleonymos and pleaded for clemency (Xen. *Hell.* 5.4.25-33, with hints of other aspects of patronage in this story at 6.4.13-14).

Many features of life in Classical Sparta look at first sight like primitive survivals from the archaic past, though we must always reckon with the possibility that an institution may have been adapted or indeed invented as part of a conscious process of archaising. A common feature of traditional societies is the rite of passage (ritual of transition to adulthood) in which adolescent males are sent into the countryside for a period before returning to the community as adults. Plutarch mentions the *krypteia* (lit., 'that which is hidden', *Lycurgus* 28), which resembles such an institution, except that for him those involved formed a secret service with the task of killing potential helot trouble-makers.

The transition from boy to man was generally less marked at Sparta than in many *poleis*. There was no equivalent of the Athenian *koureôtis* (cf. below), a ceremony in which hair was cut and dedicated to mark the end of boyhood; indeed, Spartans wore their hair long, especially in battle (Xen. *Lak.Pol.* 11.3). Nor did adulthood give a young man the right to privacy. Even newly married men, according to Xenophon (*Lak.Pol.* 1.5), were supposed to live apart from their wives. Two passages in Plutarch (*Lycurgus* 24, 25) are generally taken to imply that married together with unmarried men continued to live in barracks until the age of 30.

Throughout adult life Spartan men were expected to dine together, not with their families. Indeed, the necessary qualification for exercising full citizen rights as a Spartiate was membership of what other Greeks called a *sussition* or 'dining club'. The Spartans themselves used the Doric dialect-variant *phidition* (Aristotle, *Politics*, 2.9 = 1271a27), or alternatively the revealingly military title *suskania* ('shared tent', Xen. *Hell.* 5.3.20). On one level, this institution can be seen as an egalitarian adaptation of the symposium (drinking club) which had formed the basis of social, political and cultural life for the Archaic Greek aristocrat. Eating together (Sparta disapproved of excessive drinking, Xen. *Lak.Pol.* 5.4) was a social leveller. On the other hand, it may also have served to emphasise social divisions. Membership was by election on reaching adulthood. Plutarch (*Lycurgus* 12) reports that the vote among existing members had to be unanimous. We do not know what happened to those who were black-balled. They may have been entitled to apply for a less prestigious *sussition* which was prepared to accept them. Alternatively, they may have lost their citizen rights and became *hupomeiones* ('inferiors'), as did those who became too poor to pay their contributions. The latter point is emphasised by Aristotle among his criticisms of the Spartan system (*Politics* 2.9 = 1271a27-32).

What emerges most clearly from this survey of Spartan social institutions is the care taken to build up loyalty to the group as opposed to the family. The same motive can be seen in the rules about marriage. The status of women at Sparta was exceptional in many ways. The fact that they could inherit property in their own right distressed Aristotle, since in his view it was the tendency of rich heiresses to attract rich husbands which had led to the progressive concentration of wealth in ever-fewer hands (on this see further ch. 6). The fact that they received a formal education is highlighted in our sources, not least because it seems to have been as athletic if not as military as that of Spartan boys, and female nudity attracted prurient interest (Plutarch *Lycurgus* 14).

Spartan attitudes to marriage appear complicated. On the one hand, as we have seen, the couple were expected to live apart at least initially; and Plutarch reports odd wedding customs involving cross-dressing, ceremonial seizure, and above all secrecy (*Lycurgus* 15). On the other hand, there may be evidence that the only people allowed grave-stones were women who died in child-birth and men who died in battle (Plut. *Lycurgus* 27, though the text is disputed). If true, this would suggest that the procreation of children was being put on a level with the military needs of the *polis*. Such a restriction on gravestones would have had the incidental effect of restricting the commemoration of ancestors generally, an important form of family cult in other *poleis*. Presumably it was to encourage procreation that private arrangements for wife-swapping were permitted and widespread (Xenophon *Lak.Pol.*1.7-8). Nevertheless, the marital arrangements at least of kings at Sparta were a matter in which the state was entitled to interfere. King Arkhidamos II is even said to have been fined by the ephors for marrying a small wife, on the grounds that 'she will bear us not kings but kinglets' (Plutarch *Agesilaos* 2): the story may well be apocryphal, but the underlying assumption is that the ephors had the right to do this.

Becoming an Athenian

Whereas the education of Spartan girls was to some extent based on that of boys, Athens had a more explicit differentiation between male and female, and it began at an early age. Some events, admittedly, took place whatever the child's sex. The *dekatê* or tenth-day feast, for instance, apparently a naming ceremony, is attested for baby girls as well as boys. Ceremonies connected with organisations within the *polis*, however, seem to be restricted to males. We have already discussed (in ch. 3) the establishment of the demes or civil parishes of Attica. After Cleisthenes, c. 510 BC, a citizen was in principle a man whose name had been registered at age 18 as a member of his father's deme (women were not members). Demes, however, were for adults. More significant for the process of growing up were the phratries (lit. 'brotherhoods'), which were religious cult-groups based on nominal kinship. Our sources nowhere make explicit that every Athenian belonged to a phratry, but the phratries are so basic to Athenian identity that this is generally thought to be the case. Membership of the *genos*, on the other hand, another type of cult-group, was distinctively aristocratic and often associated with a particular family priesthood, like the Eumolpidai and the Kerukes, who between them were in charge of the Eleusinian Mysteries.

Closely associated with the phratries is an important annual festival, the Apatouria: its etymology, 'those who share the same fathers', has obvious affinities with the idea of 'brotherhood'. This festival marked several stages in the process of growing up. It was at the Apatouria that boys were presented to the phratry in early infancy, though there is contradictory evidence for the precise age. (We hear on one occasion of a girl being presented, but this may have been exceptional, because the law-court speeches do not use the fact of having been presented to prove the legitimate status of Athenian women, as they routinely do of men.) The last of the three days of the festival was the *koureôtis*, when young men on the verge of manhood had the ceremonial haircut to which we have already referred. Indeed, the mythical origins of the festival are closely connected with the status of ephebe, which was formalised or reconstituted in the 330s BC as a two-year period of military training which every hoplite or even perhaps every citizen was required to undertake between the ages of 18 and 20.

Boys, then, progressed into adult citizenship through a series of rituals. This was not true of girls. One of Aristophanes' female choruses (*Lysistrata* 641-7) claims to have progressed from carrying the sacred objects at the Arrhephoria at age 7, to 'grinding the grain for the goddess' at age 10, to serving as a 'Bear' in the cult of Artemis, before finally (but still before adulthood) serving as basket-bearer at the Panathenaia. These, however, are things done not by every girl but by a very few chosen individuals. They are designed to fulfil the religious needs of the city, rather than to mark stages in the process of growing up.

There has been considerable recent debate about the extent to which Athenian girls, or for that matter adult women, lived sheltered or secluded lifestyles. A lot is said in our sources about respectable women not being seen in public (this of course refers to the leisured classes, for as Aristotle *Politics* 4.15 = 1300a7 remarked, 'nobody could prevent the wives of the poor from going outdoors'). It has been suggested, however, that this should be interpreted as a code with an implied exclusion clause – 'respectable women are never seen out of doors (except for good cause)' – in which the definition of what constituted good cause might be infinitely flexible.

In a world almost completely without religious virginity – there were no nunneries in Classical Athens – marriage was the only respectable destiny for a woman. The distribution of power within marriage will have been affected by age-differences between husband and wife. There is some evidence that the typical age of first marriage for men was about 30 and for women about 15. The ancient world, however, had significant premature mortality, and divorce at Athens was available for women (at least if they had the consent of their male kin) as well as for men. We should not ignore the possibility of very different power relationships in second marriages.

Athenian literature was written by men for men, and surviving genres reflect the public world of men rather than the private, indoor world of women. This may distort our perspective on Athenian women. In lawcourt speeches, a respectable Athenian woman during her lifetime is always described as somebody's wife or daughter, because to name her would be an insult. A dead woman, however, was above such insults; and whereas surviving grave stelai (commemorative stones) from the Archaic period exist only for men, women as well as men are regularly named on stones from c. 440 BC onwards (see fig. 11).

The processes involved in becoming a slave or metic at Athens were very different from those involved in becoming Athenian. (It should, of course, be admitted that the process of becoming a helot or *perioikos* at Sparta may have been equally distinctive, but of that no traces remain in our sources.) Visitors to Athens had to register as metics if they stayed for more than a short period (probably 30 days). To register, they must have a citizen as *prostatês* or guarantor; as metics, they must pay a special metic-tax, the *metoikion*. The duties of the *prostatês* are unknown, though his existence clearly symbolised the subordinate status of the metic.

The implications of the *metoikion* are more complex, because taxes at Athens took various forms. Rich citizens, as well as rich metics,

Fig. 11 Grave-Stele of Ampharete, c. 410 BC. [This is one of the best preserved of many Classical stelai in which women are named. The name Ampharete appears at the top of the stele, followed by a poem identifying the baby as her dead grandchild.]

were liable to 'liturgies' (the obligation to sponsor e.g. the production of a play at a drama festival), but this was an honour as well as a burden. In Greek eyes, however, only the subjects of a tyrant paid regular, direct, personal taxes like the *metoikion* (Athenian citizens certainly did not), and it was therefore another symbol of the metics' subordinate status. The *metoikion* was a financial burden also: we are told that it was set at a drachma per month for men and half that figure for women, which implies that at least some metic women (perhaps those living independently) appeared on a list of tax-payers. This is interesting, because no citizen woman appeared on any official list. Differentiation between the sexes at Athens seems to be more marked among citizens than among non-citizens.

Solon (c. 590 BC) had banned the enslavement of Athenians at Athens, and it was thought highly improper to enslave other Greeks. Our best evidence for slave origins is the fragments of the Attic Stelai, a set of inscriptions recording auctions of confiscated property after the Herms and Mysteries scandals in 415 BC. In total 43 slaves are listed, in varying combinations of name (23 slaves), occupation (8 slaves) and ethnic origin (32 slaves, plus a further 3 described as 'born in the house', a category regarded as especially faithful). Of the 32 whose ethnic origin is recorded, one may be from a Greek community (Messenia, i.e., perhaps a former helot), one is from the marginal kingdom of Macedon, and 30 are from outside the Greek world. We cannot be sure, however, that this sample is representative.

Fig. 12 Fragment of the Attic Stelai, c. 413 BC. [The name '*Alkibiado*' can be read just below the middle of this fragment: this is not the famous Alcibiades, but a close relative. Below this are a number of slaves (*andrapoda*), identified by name and ethnic origin, and including three Thracians and a Skythian.]

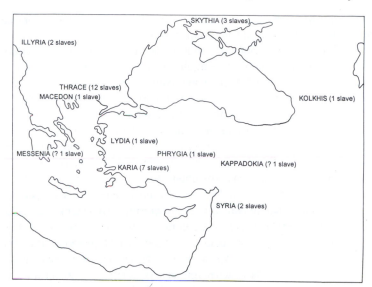

Fig. 13 Ethnic Origins of the Slaves in the Attic Stelai. [Nearly all the 32 slaves in this sample come from outside the Greek world, the majority of them from north or east. The question marks indicate slaves whose place of origin is probable rather than certain.]

A bride at Athens was welcomed into her new home by having nuts thrown over her (*katakhusma*, the ancient equivalent of confetti). Aristophanes (*Wealth* 768-9) implies that the same was done to a slave, but only to one newly purchased. Presumably the ritual serves to distinguish between those who join the household by birth and those who do so at a later date. Slaves are in a sense lifelong children. Even an adult slave can be addressed as *pais* ('boy'), but parallels in the treatment of slaves and children at Athens should not be exaggerated, because there are things that you can legitimately do to your slave (judicial torture, sexual exploitation) which you are not supposed to do to your children.

We know less than we would like about the religious involvement of slaves and metics in Athenian cults. In a range of sources, sometimes of dubious reliability, slaves are explicitly said to have been excluded from certain festivals and to have been present at others, with a third group of festivals about which nothing is said either way. It is tempting to suggest a pattern in which slaves participate in festivals of the household (Kronia) and of agriculture (Anthesteria), but not those which focus on citizenship (Apatouria) or Athens as a political community (Panathenaia, Synoikia). Difficulties, however, remain: for instance, how are we to interpret the fact that at least some publicly-owned slaves were initiated into the Eleusinian Mysteries? Metics, on the other hand, were given a special task in the Panathenaic procession as carriers of offerings (*skaphêphoroi*), dressed distinctively in purple rather than white like the citizens involved.

We hear of various imported cults in fifth- and fourth-century Athens. In an inscription of 333/2 BC, an association of import traders from the Phoenician city of Kition in Cyprus are granted land on which to build a temple for their own cult of Aphrodite (i.e. Astarte); the inscription notes a precedent, in the form of an Egyptian temple to Isis. A festival of the Thracian goddess Bendis was introduced at Athens early enough to be mentioned in Plato's *Republic* (written c. 380 BC). It may have been established on the initiative of slaves or former slaves. We do not, however, hear of religious associations designed to give former slaves a stake in society (after the manner of the *Seviri Augustales* in imperial Rome), perhaps because former slaves at Athens were not perceived as a significant social problem, or even as a distinct social group.

In Greek mythology, Spartans were descended from Dorian invaders, whereas the ancestors of the Athenians were themselves autochthonous (lit. 'born from the soil'). These two myths were powerfully expressed in where the various status-groups lived in the two societies. Ownership of land at Athens was reserved to citizens. Metics, except those who had been granted the rare privilege of *enktêsis* (lit. 'ownership', i.e. of land in a foreign *polis*), had to rent even their houses. In theory, though of course this was not always true in practice, Athenians viewed themselves as farmers – gentleman farmers if rich, or else peasant proprietors – leaving crafts to be pursued by metics. The extent to which slaves were used in Athenian agriculture is disputed, and there is evidence for citizens living in the city and walking out to their fields, but we may suspect that (with the exception of the silver-mines at Laureion, manned almost entirely by slaves) the work performed by slaves and metics was disproportionately concentrated in Athens itself and in Piraeus (the city's port).

Land belonging to Spartan citizens, on the other hand, was cultivated by helots, who presumably lived either in villages or on the Spartiates' estates. *Perioikoi*, judging from their name, 'lived round about' rather than in Sparta itself. Spartiates themselves were absentee landlords, based for much of their life in barracks in and around Sparta (which raises questions about how they supervised their estates and their helots). They extracted their living from the land which their ancestors had mythologically conquered, but they despised farming. King Kleomenes, for instance, is said by Plutarch to have described Homer's epics as poetry for Spartans, because it encouraged men to make war – while the sub-epic poet Hesiod was fit for helots, because he taught farming (*Spartan Sayings* 223a).

Chapter 5
Thucydides and the Peloponnesian War

The Inventor of the War

What we call the Peloponnesian War was a conflict (or series of conflicts) between Sparta and Athens, who started on roughly equal terms, each at the head of its confederacy of subject-allies. In all the War lasted 27 years from 431 to 404 BC, but it comprised two separate phases of fighting both of roughly ten years. The first one is known as the Arkhidamian War (431-421), after the Spartan king Arkhidamos who led the annual invasions of Attica which characterised it. Formally speaking, the Peace of Nicias in 422/1 constituted a draw, on the basis that each side would restore any territorial gains made over the previous ten years. However, its terms were never fully carried out, and cold peace gave way to full-scale hostilities in 413. The final decade of fighting is variously known as the Dekeleian War (because the Spartans this time established a permanent fortified base at Dekeleia in Attica) or as the Ionian War (because the decisive battles took place at sea off the Ionian coast of Asia Minor). It ended with the unconditional surrender of Athens in 404.

More than any other war in history, the Peloponnesian War owes its existence to its historian Thucydides. Indeed, he may with pardonable exaggeration be described as its inventor. Had it not been for him, there would have been no reason to associate these two conflicts together as 'the' Peloponnesian War, to the exclusion of an earlier period of fighting between the same combatants c. 461-c. 446 BC (modern scholars have sometimes labelled this the 'First Peloponnesian War', but the term has never really caught on). Why two wars (c. 461-c. 446 and 431-404) rather than one (c. 461-404) or three (c. 461-c. 446, 431-421, 413-404)?

What little we know about Thucydides derives from his work. He gives us a few details at the start (1.1) and rather more in the so-called Second Preface (5.26):

> Thucydides the Athenian wrote the history of this period, by summers and winters as each event happened, down to the time the Spartans put an end to Athenian power and occupied Piraeus and the Long Walls. By then, the War had lasted 27 years in

all.... I lived through the whole of it, being old enough to follow what was happening, and paying close attention so that I could understand it clearly.

(Thucydides, 5.26)

He is claiming here to have been old enough in 431 to realise the importance of the War at its outset; he must indeed have been aged at least 23, because he goes on to mention that he served as general at Amphipolis in 424, and there seems to have been a minimum age of thirty for this, as for many other public offices. He cannot have been much older, because his discussion of the precise duration of the War implies that he was alive when it ended in 404. On the other hand, he may not have outlived it by much, not least because his account of the War is clearly incomplete. His history consists of a long introduction (book 1), followed by a narrative of the first twenty years of the War itself (books 2-8), organised year-by-year into an eight-month summer (i.e. the campaigning season) and a four-month winter.

Thucydides intended his account to continue down to 404, and at 5.26 he claims to have achieved this. Our version however breaks off (8.109) while describing the events of year twenty-one (411 BC), and the fact that Thucydides' would-be continuator Xenophon began his account at this point implies that nothing more was known in antiquity. We cannot be certain why Thucydides ends here. He may well have died leaving his work incomplete; but 8.109 was probably not the last thing he wrote, because book 8 seems to show less knowledge of the final stages of the War than do some other portions of the text, most notably the Second Preface, which as we saw cannot have been written before 404. We seem to be dealing not just with an incomplete text, but with one that has been incompletely revised.

Classical scholars have traditionally concentrated on the composition of particular literary works, although the fact that ancient audiences enjoyed the *Iliad* (for instance) as a unity is in many ways more significant than the question of how it came into existence. In the case of a patently incomplete work like Thucydides' history, however, the existence of different strata of composition is an important issue. Thucydides is generally a consistent author but there are a number of striking contradictions, often where an analytical judgment at one point in the text is not borne out in the detailed narrative elsewhere. It is possible in some cases that Thucydides was in the process of changing his mind, though such explanations cannot be demonstrated and should not perhaps be over-used.

Thucydides is one of the most important but also one of the most difficult of ancient writers. Difficulty arises because his meaning is often unclear. Controversy surrounds the programmatic statement about the use of speeches:

> I have made the various speakers say what seemed to me to be most suitable for the given occasion, while sticking as closely as possible to the general gist of what was actually said.
>
> (Thucydides, 1.22)

Is he claiming here to report what was said or what should have been said, and what is the relationship between reporting the gist and inventing the details? Speeches are common in ancient works of history (though ancient writers rarely bother to justify using them); Thucydides' speeches are in places linguistically incomprehensible, with extensive abstract generalisations about power and the human predicament. But even in the narrative, as we saw in chapter 2 with the revolt of Naxos, there are times when he manipulates language with the apparent intention of imposing a viewpoint on his readers.

Thucydides rarely states a personal view, but strong emotions underlie the calm surface and his personality dominates his text. Nor does he tell us how he knows what he knows. Despite his insistence on eye-witness evidence (1.22), he virtually never mentions his informants, presumably because to do so would be to admit that his conclusions are the result of a process of inference rather than statements of fact. Thucydides dominates the Peloponnesian War not least because his suppression of his sources has made it impossible to construct an alternative account.

What makes Thucydides important is his influence. At first sight, he matches our popular image of the ideal historian (admittedly an image based on nineteenth-century readings of Thucydides himself): he offers not social analysis but political and military narrative; he has a fetish for precise dates; and he claims to record fact rather than subjective opinion. It is Thucydides, moreover, who has fixed in the minds of all subsequent readers down to the present day the conviction that the Peloponnesian War is the central event in Greek history (as witnessed in the choice of *Athens and Sparta* as the subject for a book in this series), and it is his portrayal of individual characters which causes Kleon to be regarded for all time as the pattern of a rabble-rousing demagogue, Alcibiades to be seen as a flamboyantly traitorous maverick, and Pericles to be the hero of what is often if misleadingly known as Periclean Athens.

To speak of 'the Peloponnesian War' is to assume an Athenian perspective. Spartans saw things differently, and it is to highlight this that several recent works on Spartan history have substituted the phrase 'the Athenian War'. Thucydides calls it 'the War of the Peloponnesians and the Athenians', which constitutes a claim to impartiality. Impartiality however is in practice unattainable: he could not avoid being the Athenian general who had been exiled after the failure of his command at Amphipolis. His only comment on this episode (that exile gave him better facilities for gathering information from the Spartan side, 5.26) is just a little bit too dispassionate to be true, especially given his difficulties in extracting information from the Spartans (5.68, discussed in ch. 1).

Thucydides' personal circumstances do not in themselves entitle us to regard him as a partisan either of Athens or for that matter of Sparta. Because he rarely offers an explicit opinion, his views have been the subject of continuing debate. For what it is worth, my own opinion is that he is no great admirer of the Spartans (they are portrayed as duplicitous, e.g. 3.68, and also as strategically over-cautious, 8.96), but that his view of Athens is more complex. The heroisation of Pericles, who died in the third year of the War, serves to construct a nostalgic image of an ideal Athens as a stick with which to beat contemporary Athenian political leaders (most clearly seen in the obituary of Pericles at 2.65).

The Causes of War

Thucydides creates two problems: what is he saying? and is he right? In general, the first question has traditionally preoccupied scholars. The second is more radical and until recently has rarely been asked. Earlier scholars looked for Thucydides' opinion about Athenian imperialism, for instance, believing that he must have known what it was like. Discussion focused on the apparent gap between assertions that it was unpopular (Thuc. 2.8) and specific instances of unexpected loyalty (Thuc. 7.82). Now however there is widespread acceptance that Thucydides' aristocratic friends among the allies are likely to have been more hostile to Athens than the mass of their poor fellow-citizens, and that this may have distorted his view.

On the important question of why the War was fought, this situation is reversed. There are two highly influential theories put forward by recent scholars: Kagan believes that Thucydides' analysis of the causes of the War (1.23) is wrong, and proposes an alternative explanation; Ste Croix, on the other hand, believes that Thucydides is right, but that he has been universally misunderstood. The paradox is that in this case it is Ste Croix whose views are more contentious and more wide-ranging.

Before we discuss Ste Croix and Kagan, one older theory deserves mention in passing: Cornford in *Thucydides Mythistoricus* (1907) argued that the War was forced on Pericles by Athenian merchants keen to break Corinth's stranglehold on trade through the Gulf of Corinth to the rich markets of Sicily and Southern Italy. Thucydides, according to Cornford, knew this but suppressed it, because it would have undermined the epic scope of his history. Cornford's approach to Thucydides was radical before its time. In so far as ancient states had a trade policy, however, it was about securing supplies of food and certain scarce resources, not about export markets. Moreover, mercantile interests do not seem to have significantly influenced Athenian policy, not least because many of the merchants based at Athens were metics rather than citizens and so had no votes. It is because of his anachronistic views on trade that Cornford's theory is rejected by modern scholars.

Thucydides (1.23) distinguishes between the 'truest but least publicised *prophasis* (explanation)' and the 'openly expressed *aitiai* (reasons or complaints)' on both sides. The former category he immediately glosses as follows, with unusual emphasis on his own opinion: 'I believe that the Athenians, by becoming powerful and inspiring fear on

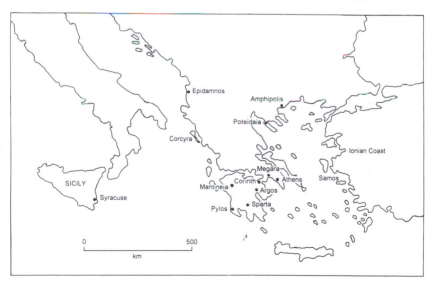

Fig. 14 The Peloponnesian War. [The places named on this map are chosen to illustrate the discussion in the text of the Causes of the War, and also the brief summary of the Course of the War in the final section of this chapter.]

the part of the Spartans, compelled them to go to war'. In the second category he places three disputes which blew up in the period 435-432, and which he proceeds to describe: the quarrels over Epidamnos (1.24-30), Corcyra (1.31-55) and Poteidaia (1.56-65). It is ironic that Thucydides insists on the definitive status of his discussion, after which 'nobody will ever again have to enquire how such a great war came upon the Greeks' (1.23), because the passage has created endless controversy.

For Kagan, as for many predecessors, the distinction between *aitia* and *prophasis* is between immediate and underlying causes. He regards Thucydides' proposed *prophasis*, however, as demonstrably false: the growth of Athenian power might have explained the outbreak of the First Peloponnesian War in c. 461 BC, but by the 430s Athens had visibly stopped expanding. Indeed, the search for an underlying explanation is in Kagan's view misconceived, because he believes that the War happened by accident, as the result of a series of diplomatic miscalculations. He thinks that the Corinthians interfered at Corcyra because they did not expect the Athenians to react, and that the Athenians imposed an unnecessarily harsh ultimatum on Poteidaia without realising how this would frighten the Spartan alliance. Nobody, on this view, wanted war. They all blundered into it by mistake, in much the same way as the Great Powers did in certain interpretations of 1914.

Ste Croix sees the two nouns *prophasis* and *aitia* as simple linguistic variants. In his view the distinction is between real but secret reasons and those which are put forward in public. (This interpretation is now generally accepted.) He further argues that 'compelled' (*anankasai*, 1.23) is used in a weak sense, and need only mean that the Spartans felt obliged to take action. Traditionally this passage has been taken to mean that the Spartans formally started the War but that they were really reacting to Athenian pressure; Ste Croix turns Sparta into the real as well as the formal aggressor. (This has met with a mixed response.)

He continues with an elaborate reinterpretation of the decrees directed against Megara (neighbour of Athens and ally of Sparta). These constitute a notorious silence in Thucydides, who mentions them only in passing (e.g. 1.139), whereas Plutarch (*Pericles* 29-30), following Aristophanes (*Acharnians* 530-9), sees them as a major cause of war. One of the decrees seems to have banned Megarian citizens from entering the Athenian *agora* and the harbours of the Athenian Empire, which has traditionally been interpreted as an economic blockade and as deliberate provocation. Ste Croix argues that this decree was simply a response to religious impiety, that its scope was limited, and that it was never a serious diplomatic issue. Plutarch, on this view, has simply swallowed a piece of Aristophanic fantasy.

This interpretation has some attractive features. Aristophanes' decree is certainly phrased as a parody of a traditional drinking song, and it is immediately linked to a particularly outrageous fantasy, in which the origins of the War are traced back to the theft of three prostitutes (*Acharnians* 523-9, a clear parody of Herodotus 1.1-4). Overall, however, Ste Croix has rather too much to gain from playing down the significance of the Megarian decrees. It enables him to redeem the reputation of Thucydides while leaving responsibility in the hands of Sparta. Moreover, this final stage of his argument requires some rather elaborate special pleading about markets and harbours. (It has not generally won favour.)

The Course of the War

Warfare on land was conservative. For several centuries it had been based on hoplites or heavy infantrymen, armed with thrusting-spears and shields designed for formation-fighting. Hoplites were those who could afford their own armour (including prosperous peasant farmers, and perhaps the richest 50% of the population). They fought as a part-time militia, and training was minimal: Sparta alone maintained its citizens as professional soldiers, whose ability to hold formation and perform simple manoeuvres had left them with at least the reputation of being undefeatable in pitched battles. On uneven ground, hoplites were vulnerable to attack by light-armed troops. Hoplite warfare, however, continued to dominate Greek military strategy, partly because war was fought over relatively sparse agricultural land, and partly for reasons of social prejudice. Everybody knew that those who could afford their armour were superior to those who could not.

Athens' naval power relied on the trireme, rowed by a paid crew of 200 free men (citizens, metics or allies), who could not afford hoplite armour. The initial aim had been to recreate a land battle at sea, by grappling an enemy ship to board it with hoplite marines. By the 430s, however, Athens was using the trained skill of its crews to manoeuvre into positions where they could ram or disable their opponents, at least on the open sea. Phormion's victories in the Corinthian gulf (Thuc. 2.84, 2.90-2) illustrate some of the tactics that could be attempted.

Siege weapons were rudimentary (see for details Thuc. 2.71-8), and without internal dissension there was no prospect of storming any but the smallest city. But most Greek *poleis* had a subsistence economy and to lose the harvest could be crippling. Sparta planned to invade Attica in time for harvest, allowing the army to live off the land for the few weeks needed to wreck the crops: eventually their opponents would have to fight and inevitably lose a pitched battle. At the outset, it was widely expected that this might take a couple of years (Thuc. 7.28). In the event, invasions were repeated more or less annually until 425, without obvious success.

The Athenians responded with a policy associated with Pericles. They evacuated the countryside of Attica, using the city's wealth and its ships to ensure supplies, and moving the people into Athens itself and the area protected since the 450s by the Long Walls leading from the city to the port of Piraeus. Meanwhile they responded with naval raids on Spartan allies, and from 424 on Lakonia itself. Sparta had entered the War to 'free the Greeks from [Athenian] slavery' (Thuc. 2.8), and had to win decisively to maintain prestige and control of its subject-allies.

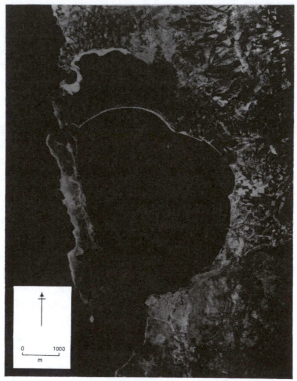

Fig. 15 Aerial photograph of Pylos and Sphakteria. [Sphakteria is the island, and Pylos is the rocky headland immediately north of it. The fact that Thucydides gets the measurements wrong (the southern entrance to the bay is far wider, and the island much longer, than he says at 4.8) suggests that despite his reputation for accuracy, his account here relies on hearsay.]

Two unforeseen problems marred the otherwise successful Athenian strategy. Over-crowding in Athens during the second year's invasion precipitated a plague which devastated Athenian manpower and morale (it is the effect on morale which particularly interests Thucydides, Thuc. 2.47-55). Moreover, to maintain a fleet was expensive, particularly when allies revolted and had to be starved out (Thuc. 2.70 says that the seige of Poteidaia in 432-430/29 cost 2,000 talents). From 429/8 there were efforts to cut expenditure, if we can judge from the loans to the state from the sanctuary of Athene Polias, which drop from over 1,000 talents per year to an average of 200 talents. In 428/7 the Athenians introduced an emergency war-tax, raising 200 talents (Thuc. 3.19). In 425/4 we have a decree, not mentioned by Thucydides, raising the tribute assessment from c. 600 talents to some 1,460 talents.

Fig. 16 Athenian Dedication of Spartan Shield captured at Pylos in 425 BC. [This was dedicated in the Stoa Poikile at Athens, with the following inscription: 'The Athenians, from the Lakedaimonians (i.e., Spartans) at Pylos'. The lettering on the original photograph consists of light grey dots, and is barely visible. The black dots are an approximation, and are taken from a drawing prepared by the excavators.]

It was in an attempt to break this dangerous deadlock that the Athenian general Demosthenes (not the later orator) achieved the first spectacular success of the War in 425. He fortified the headland of Pylos in Messenia as a raiding-base, and together with Kleon he used light-armed troops to break up a Spartan hoplite force sent against him, which had unwisely trapped itself on the irregular terrain of the island of Sphakteria (Thuc. 4.1-41). No fewer than 120 of the reputedly invincible Spartiates were captured – a massive blow to Spartan manpower and prestige.

Athens could not sustain the initiative and suffered a comparable blow in 424, when the Spartan Brasidas with an irregular army slipped into Thrace and induced the revolt of several Athenian allies, including the major city of Amphipolis (Thuc. 4.75-88, 4.102-16). Following a one-year truce (from Spring 423), Kleon's attempt to recover the city ended with his defeat and death, but also that of the victorious Brasidas (Thuc. 5.2-11). This removed 'the two people on each side most opposed to peace' (Thuc. 5.16), and the Peace of Nicias was agreed in autumn 422 (Thuc. 5.18-19).

Scholars disagree over who gained more from the Peace. Materially it was Sparta, because although Pylos and Amphipolis were not in the event handed back, they did recover their 120 Spartiates. Their failure to win conclusively, however, created tensions. Several allies seceded, joining Sparta's traditional Peloponnesian rival Argos. Had the allies received more help from Athens (by now openly hostile to Sparta), the Spartans might have lost rather than narrowly winning the critical battle at Mantineia in 418.

The initiative was in Athenian hands, and they sought to achieve a decisive advantage through a massive expedition to Sicily (415-413 BC, with a full account in Thuc. 6-7). Preparations at Athens were interrupted by major religious scandals (the mutilation of the Herms and the profanation of the Mysteries), which led to the recall of Alcibiades, one of the appointed generals, who fled to Sparta. The expedition lost momentum, and its eventual and total loss provoked widespread revolts among Athens' subject-allies in the winter of 413/12.

Sparta meanwhile had been persuaded (by Alcibiades, according to Thuc. 6.88-93) to attack Athens on its own terms. This would need ships and a permanent base in Attica, and that meant money. Thucydides (4.50) implies in passing that Persian money had for years been on offer, but that Sparta had previously hesitated because the price was Persian rule over the Greek cities of Ionia, which would undermine the Spartan claim to be fighting to free the Greeks. By 412/11, however, they were driven to accept (though there are difficulties involved in interpreting Thucydides' three alleged Spartan/Persian treaties, 8.18, 8.36-7, 8.57-8), thus creating a diplomatic contradiction which will be explored further in chapter 6.

The Athenians were desperate, and in 411 agreed to suspend democracy in favour of an oligarchic regime of Four Hundred, who (it was said) would conduct the War better. (This is the last detailed episode in Thucydides, 8.45-98, and we have a unique chance to compare the rival account in *Ath.Pol.* 29-33.) It soon became clear that the real aim of the Four Hundred was a sell-out, and their regime collapsed within four months. A moderate oligarchy of Five Thousand took over, and achieved relative harmony with the fleet (which was based at Samos and had declared democratic independence) before full democracy was restored in 410.

After this we rely chiefly on Xenophon's more patchy account (*Hell.* 1.1-2.2). In 410-407 a number of revolting allies were recovered by the Athenians under the diplomatic and military leadership of Alcibiades, now recalled, but dismissed into a final exile after a skirmish at Notion in 407. The Spartans were held back by disputes between their naval commanders Lysander and Kallikratidas, which may have contributed to the latter's death in Athens' final Pyrrhic victory at Arginoussai (406). In 405 Lysander caught the Athenian fleet at anchor at Aigospotamoi. Athens was besieged through the winter and surrendered the following spring. As the price of victory, Sparta imposed another oligarchy – the Thirty, later known as the Thirty Tyrants – but that belongs after the War in chapter 6.

Chapter 6
A Land Fit for Heroes?

Recovery and Decline

Paradoxically, winning the Peloponnesian War did more long-term damage to Sparta than losing did to Athens. That seemed unlikely in 404 BC, when Spartan success appeared as total as Athenian defeat. Nevertheless, within 50 years, Athens (even if never as potent as in the fifth century) was again a great power, and Sparta was not.

Several factors underlie the decline of Sparta. Spartan foreign policy displayed unforced errors (in the treatment of their Peloponnesian War allies) and unavoidable diplomatic contradictions (in their relationship with Persia). At home, there was disunity among the governing elite, and the structural weakness of declining citizen manpower.

Athenian recovery is harder to explain. In 404 the Spartan admiral Lysander turned Athens into a satellite state. The Athenians had to give up the empire and most of their fleet, to become subject-allies of Sparta, and to accept an oligarchic puppet government, the Thirty, who stayed in power through the winter of 404/3. The Thirty's failure was partly the result of the unpopularity created by their purges, which earned them a reputation as the 'Thirty Tyrants': they are said to have killed as many Athenians in eight months as the Spartans had killed in ten years of war (Xen. *Hell*. 2.4.21). In part it was the result of luck, as when a freak snowstorm stopped them defeating the democratic counter-revolutionaries led by Thrasyboulos. But it was also the result of power-play at Sparta.

Faced by Thrasyboulos' initial success, the Thirty appealed to Sparta, and Lysander had himself appointed to sort out the situation at Athens, presumably by re-establishing the Thirty in power. After he had gone, King Pausanias brought about a shift in Spartan policy: he himself went to Athens and restored the democracy, subject to the protection of a General Amnesty for all former supporters of the oligarchs, except the Thirty themselves and a few specified adherents. Athenian sources regard the Amnesty as a success and as a triumph of democratic magnanimity. Certainly outright civil strife was avoided, but there were a lot of pinpricks and some show trials (which may provide a context for the trial of Socrates in 399 BC). The fact that the Amnesty did have some success may have been due in part to fear of Spartan retaliation.

Pausanias was put on trial and narrowly acquitted following his return to Sparta, which suggests that there were considerable conflicts over policy. His motives in 403 are hard to determine. He may have feared Lysander's power, but there were also diplomatic considerations. It is notable that Sparta's ally Thebes, after voting to destroy Athens in 404 (Xen. *Hell.* 2.2.19), nevertheless helped Thrasyboulos in 403 (Xen. *Hell.* 2.4.1). Evidently Thebes distrusted the Thirty as Lysander's puppets, but there was also more general allied dissatisfaction at the way in which Sparta was monopolizing the fruits of victory. Pausanias may have been afraid of Sparta's reputation being damaged.

If so, he was far-sighted. Within eight years, Sparta's leading allies Thebes and Corinth had joined Argos and their former enemy Athens in revolt against Sparta, thereby beginning the Corinthian War (395-387). For the Spartans this was a diplomatic disaster, and what sparked it off was Sparta's attack on Persia. It was Persian money which had allowed Sparta to win the final phase of the Peloponnesian War in 413-404, but in c. 400 the Spartans invaded Asia Minor, which seemed a good if cynical way of recovering lost prestige. As we saw in chapter 5, Sparta had begun the Peloponnesian War promising to free the Greeks from slavery to Athens; they had achieved this only by selling the Greek cities of Ionia to Persia; now they could claim that their real aim had been to unite Greece in preparation for an anti-Persian crusade. This pan-hellenic ('all-Greek', i.e., anti-Persian) agenda is clear in 396, when King Agesilaos took command of Spartan forces: like Agamemnon in the myth, he made a sacrifice at Aulis near Thebes before attacking Asia. However, the officials of the Theban-dominated Boiotian League were unimpressed by this appeal to the rhetoric of the Trojan War:

> When they heard that he was sacrificing, they sent horsemen telling him not to continue, and threw down the sacrifices from the altar. Agesilaos, in a fury, called on the gods as witnesses, and sailed off in his trireme.
>
> (Xenophon, *Hell.,* 3.4.3-4).

The Persian Great King saw the Spartan invasion as treacherous, and promptly offered financial assistance to Sparta's already disaffected allies. The Corinthian War, which resulted, was a messy affair. On land, a struggle of attrition gradually favoured Sparta; at sea, the allies had a notable success when a mainly Persian fleet under the Athenian commander

Konon defeated the Spartans at Knidos in 394. Konon promptly returned to Athens and, using money supplied by the Persians for the purpose, rebuilt the walls which had been destroyed in 404/3. Success, however, brought problems for the Athenians: naval campaigns under Thrasyboulos in 390/89 revived Persian fears of a restored Athenian Empire, and in 387 Sparta and Persia agreed to what is variously known as the King's Peace (after the Persian Great King) or the Peace of Antalkidas (the Spartan diplomat responsible for the negotiations) – thus clearly indicating the main beneficiaries.

The King's Peace sought to impose itself throughout the Greek world, and was the model for a series of what are called 'common' peaces. The most important clause was that apart from those in Asia Minor (which were to belong to Persia) and a few specified exceptions, all Greek *poleis* were to be *autonomoi* (self-governing). It was left to the Spartans to interpret this term, and they did so with notable self-interest: they intervened extensively in the affairs of other states, refusing for instance to let the Thebans control Boiotia, while nevertheless themselves retaining Messenia. In 382 a Spartan commander named Phoibidas occupied and garrisoned the citadel at Thebes in time of peace. The Spartans, while repudiating his action, nevertheless retained the garrison, which was not expelled until 379. A similar attempt in 378 by Sphodrias, another Spartan commander, to seize the Piraeus (the port of Athens) provides the background to one of the most important surviving inscriptions, the Charter of the Second Athenian Confederacy.

Notable features of this document, which is ignored by Xenophon, are the emphasis that this is a defensive alliance 'so that the Spartans may allow the Greeks to be free and autonomous' (lines 9-11), and the attempts to attract allies by banning Athenians from owning allied land (lines 35-41, which helps illustrate allied objections to fifth-century Athenian imperialism). Also worth noting is the range of scripts at the bottom and on the side of the stone, listing the allied states: this was a successful manifesto, and for some time new members kept joining, up to a total of more than fifty by the late 370s.

In 371 Sparta offered to renew the peace. Agesilaos insisted again on the autonomy of Boiotia, which the Theban commander Epameinondas would not accept. This looked like skilful diplomacy, because it isolated the Thebans and allowed Sparta to attack them. In the event, Epameinondas won the battle of Leuktra, which was a devastating blow to Sparta. It was not so much the battle itself, though that did cause a major diplomatic reshuffle, forcing Athens and Sparta together for a decade during which Thebes dominated the Greek world. Instead, what mattered

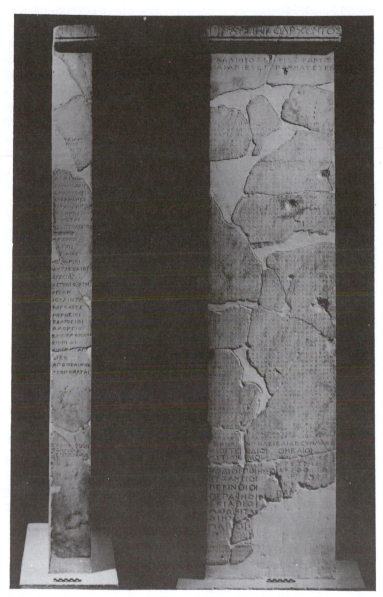

Fig. 17 The Charter of the Second Athenian Confederacy, 377 BC. [The range of scripts used on the bottom and at the side of the stele suggests that the names of new allies were added successively as they joined the alliance. The word '*autonomos*' (from one of the passages quoted in the text) can be read in line 10, two lines above the erasure.]

were the implications of Spartan defeat and the way in which the Thebans followed it up.

Aristotle, in a famous analysis (*Politics* 2.9 = 1270a15-b6), claimed that what destroyed Sparta was *oliganthrôpia* (lit. 'fewness of men'). It was not, in his view, a question of birth-rate, but of an inheritance system which concentrated wealth in the hands of the few – and we should remember what we saw in chapter 4, that those who became too poor to pay the contributions to their *sussition* (dining club) ceased to be citizens. Modern estimates of the rate of decline of citizen manpower vary (see fig. 18). What is clear is that numbers had been declining for at least a century, and that the loss of 400 Spartiates at Leuktra made the process visible and unsustainable.

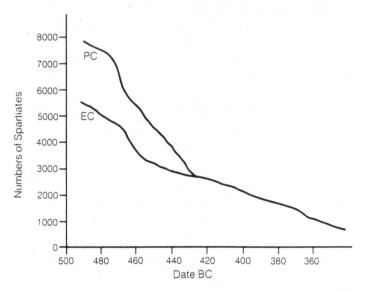

Fig. 18 The Decline in Spartan Citizen Manpower. [Estimates for the early fifth century are very speculative, and a lot depends on the scale of the losses caused by the great earthquake in the 460s. This graph gives two possible reconstructions, those of Cavaignac (EC) in 1912, and of Cartledge (PC) in 1987.]

What made decline irrevocable was Epameinondas' use of victory. Repeatedly invading the Peloponnese, he amalgamated most of the Arkadian cities in his new foundation of Megalopolis, to prevent any risk of Spartan expansion northwards. More importantly, he established Messene as an independent *polis* – thereby depriving Sparta of half its sovereign territory, and further exacerbating the manpower crisis.

Discovering Past Glories: Lycurgus at Athens

Sparta after 371 BC was never a great power, but Athens was different. Admittedly the Athenians proved unable to resist the rise of Philip of Macedon from 358, and in the end Philip succeeded in defeating the combined armies of Athens and of Thebes at the decisive land battle of Chaeronea (338), which gave him control of Greece. As a naval power, however, Athens remained important: the Athenians were able to man 170 ships when they revolted against Macedon after the death in 323 of Philip's son Alexander the Great.

One reason for Philip's initial success was that it coincided with a period of comparative Athenian weakness: despite the promises in the Charter of the Second Confederacy (above), the Athenians had gradually begun to treat their allies more and more as subjects. This had led to the Social War (i.e., war against the allies, 357-355 BC), at the end of which Athens had been forced to concede that those who wished (including important places like Byzantium, Khios, and Rhodes) could leave the alliance.

In 355, Athens was financially as well as militarily weak. One of the most striking features of the following period was the financial recovery of Athens under Euboulos (c. 355-346) and Lycurgus (c. 336-c. 324) – the latter not to be confused with the legendary Spartan law-giver of the same name. Modern readers are conditioned, partly by the accident of the survival of Demosthenes' speeches, to see the third quarter of the fourth century in terms of the struggle between Demosthenes and Philip, as witness the term 'Demosthenic Athens'. It could be argued, however, that Lycurgus in particular is a more significant figure in the history of Athens.

Both Euboulos and Lycurgus were financial reformers. Two ancient texts, neither of them very reliable, claim that Euboulos increased the annual income of the *polis* from a low point of 130 talents to a figure of 400 talents (pseudo-Demosthenes 10.37-38), roughly comparable to the level of imperial tribute in the mid fifth century; and that Lycurgus raised this to an impressive 1,200 talents (pseudo-Plutarch, *Lives of the Ten Orators*, 842f). Euboulos' main reform was apparently to reduce frivolous military expenditure by passing a law that any unbudgeted income should be stored in a reserve fund (the so-called Theoric Fund) rather than being available for the assembly to spend at will. This is an interesting move in the direction of efficiency and, perhaps, away from unrestricted democracy.

It was probably in 336 that Athens moved still further in this direction by establishing the office of superintendent of the *dioikêsis* (financial administration) – to be filled by election, not by lot, and for a four-year rather than a one-year term. It was through this post that Lycurgus for twelve years controlled Athenian finances. His task was made easier by Philip and Alexander, who throughout this period prevented Athens from having an independent foreign policy and having to pay for it. However, he is also known for his success in persuading rich Athenians voluntarily to contribute to the needs of the *polis*, and to become in a sense its financial patrons: this system of 'euergetism', or voluntary public sponsorship, is characteristic of the Hellenistic Greek city. Classical Athens, on the other hand, had been characterised by 'liturgies' (for which see ch. 4), a system of compulsory public sponsorship, imposed on rich citizens in lieu of taxation.

Lycurgus had an impact on Athens, not simply as a collector of revenue, but because of how money was spent under his direction, particularly on public buildings and other capital projects. Some of the expenditure was military, including work on the shipyards and the arsenal, and the strengthening of the navy. There were also a number of civic buildings. It is possible that the Pnyx (where the assembly met) was rebuilt and substantially enlarged at this time, though the evidence is archaeological, and it may have happened in the Roman period. About other things, we can be more certain: Lycurgus is identified in our sources, for instance, as the person responsible for constructing the Panathenaic Stadium and the Theatre of Dionysos. The latter is particularly interesting, because he is also said to have put up bronze statues of the three great fifth-century tragedians, Aeschylus, Sophocles and Euripides; and to have passed a law forcing actors who revived their plays to stick to the authorised text.

Lycurgus seems to have been particularly interested in the cultural and religious aspects of what it meant to be an Athenian citizen, and the way in which citizenship was acted out in civic festivals. As a period of public building, the age of Lycurgus rivalled that of Pericles (which was discussed in ch. 2). The difference is that the Periclean building programme was designed to glorify the present splendour of imperial Athens, whereas Lycurgus represents the beginnings of a process of fossilizing the past.

Reform and Revolution: Agis and Kleomenes at Sparta

The best attested sequence of events in Spartan history after 371 BC is the third-century revolution, initiated by the Eurypontid King Agis IV (244-241BC), and revived by his Agiad counterpart Kleomenes III (235-222). We know about these two because Plutarch made them the subject of his only pair of double biographies, paralleling the reforming Roman tribunes, Tiberius and Gaius Gracchus.

Like Tiberius Gracchus, Agis had a simple proposal: to redistribute land and cancel debts, thereby increasing the number of Spartiates and solving the manpower crisis. In other *poleis*, redistribution of land and cancellation of debts would have been a revolutionary slogan. Agis, as a good revolutionary, claimed to be restoring traditional Spartan values. Plutarch (*Agis* 5) appears to reproduce Agis' rhetoric when he asserts that the number of *klaroi* or land-holdings had remained constant (elsewhere he reports a figure of 9,000, *Lycurgus* 8) from the time of the legendary law-giver Lycurgus to that of the irresponsible ephor Epitadeus, who had allegedly passed a law allowing property to be left by will rather than from father to son. Plutarch's account is hard to match with the analysis of the Spartan inheritance system offered by Aristotle and cited in the first section of this chapter; and Epitadeus, who is suspiciously undated and otherwise unattested, has probably been invented to support Agis' propaganda.

The parallels between Plutarch's Agis and his Tiberius Gracchus are at times so close as to attract suspicion. Faced with intransigent opposition from the Agiad King Leonidas, Agis arranged to have him deposed in favour of his own ally Kleombrotos, Leonidas' son-in-law and himself a member of the Agiad royal family. There was a Spartan precedent for this: in c. 491, King Kleomenes (Agiad) had had the Eurypontid Damaratos replaced by Damaratos' distant cousin Latykhidas. But it is striking that Leonidas in Plutarch's story fulfils much the same function as Tiberius Gracchus' rival tribune Octavius, who is similarly intransigent and similarly deposed. Moreover, just as Tiberius invents a new constitutional doctrine (that tribunes, as delegates, are bound to obey the people's will), so Agis similarly invents the doctrine of conjoint royal supremacy (i.e., that if both kings are agreed, like Kleombrotos and himself, they can over-ride the ephors). In the event, however, his reforms (like those of Tiberius) were stalled: Agis' powerful but debt-ridden supporters persuaded him to abolish debts while delaying the redistribution of land, and then abandoned him.

Leonidas, who returned from exile in 241 to have Agis executed, arranged for his son Kleomenes to marry Agis' widow. According to Plutarch, his motive was that she was a substantial heiress, but the effect was to make Kleomenes sympathetic to Agis' policies (Plutarch, *Kleomenes* 1). Kleomenes, who inherited his father's throne in 235, was (like Gaius Gracchus) a far more systematic reformer than his predecessor. Instead of simply inventing a constitutional doctrine, like Agis' conjoint royal supremacy, Kleomenes revolutionised the constitution by claiming that the ephors had originally been assistants to the kings. He used this as a pretext (after first taking the precaution of assassinating the current ephors) to abolish the post, on the grounds that successive holders had abused their powers. Plutarch says that:

> Kleomenes removed the chairs of the ephors, except one, on which he himself intended to sit to conduct official business.
>
> (Plutarch, *Kleomenes*, 10)

To us, this may sound like a vaguely ridiculous action, but it was important in a society in which the symbolism of authority was powerful: the ephors alone, for instance, had had the right to remain seated when a king approached them.

Kleomenes' relations with his fellow-king were similarly revolutionary. He was not content, as Agis had been, with arranging for an alternative claimant to take the place of a deposed rival. Instead, he simply filled the Eurypontid throne with his own brother – an Agiad with no Eurypontid connections. This was in effect the abolition of the dual kingship, which was never to be restored.

Equally far-reaching was Kleomenes' success in carrying his proposals into effect. Land was redistributed to at least some *perioikoi* and helots, and Kleomenes remained in power until the Achaean commander Aratos managed to persuade Antigonos III of Macedon to intervene, on the grounds that Kleomenes' success as a reformer was making him a social as well as a military threat to Sparta's neighbours. Following his defeat by Antigonos at Sellasia in 222, Kleomenes fled into voluntary exile in Egypt, only to be killed there while resisting arrest.

The lack of sources makes it impossible to write a narrative of Spartan history after Kleomenes. We do, however, hear of one coda to this revolutionary symphony, in the person of Nabis, who ruled Sparta as a self-styled 'king' from c. 207 to 192 BC. Our evidence for Nabis consists mainly of a few (very hostile) remarks in Polybius, for whom Nabis is the model of a wicked tyrant. Nabis certainly seems to be a tyrant in the Greek sense that he had no constitutional claim to the throne, though he may have been a distant descendant of the Eurypontid King Damaratos who had fled to Persia after his deposition in c. 491. Nabis is an interesting figure, because he appears to have been responsible at least for beginning to build a city wall at Sparta. Classical Sparta, as we saw in chapter 2, was unwalled. To build a wall was to admit the possibility that Sparta might be attacked – at once a concession to reality, the rejection of a certain type of myth, and a step towards becoming a normal Hellenistic *polis*.

Chapter 7
Greece under Roman Rule

Sparta as Theme Park

The first half of the second century BC is a period of progressive Roman interference in mainland Greece. There had been surprisingly little contact between the two before 220 BC, but the threat of Macedonian support for Hannibal's invasion of Italy (218-202 BC, the Second Punic War) had drawn Rome into conflict with Macedon. For reasons that are debated, Rome in this period proved reluctant to annexe enemy territory: instead, the Romans repeatedly attacked, defeated, and destabilised their opponents in a series of three Macedonian Wars (211-205, 200-197, 171-168).

Rome fought the second and third of these conflicts with the assistance of various Greek allies hostile to Macedon, including the cities of the Achaean League (a confederacy which had been the leading power in the Peloponnese since before the defeat of Kleomenes at Sellasia in 222 BC). As time went on, the Romans demanded ever more abject support from their Greek allies. Following the settlement of 167 BC, the Romans interned a large number of leading Achaeans in Italy (where they remained until 151), on the grounds that they had not been sufficiently abject. Eventually, an Achaean revolt led to the sack of Corinth in 146. The League was abolished, and most of its cities were transferred to the Roman province of Macedonia (where they remained until the creation of Achaea, i.e. central and southern Greece, as a separate province in 27 BC).

The story of this period is told by the later Roman historian Livy, whose coverage of the second century is extant down to the settlement of 167 BC: Livy's is a fairly bland account, told from the Roman viewpoint. Less complete but more revealing is Polybius' version (covering the period 220-146, but what survives is only the first five of forty books, with excerpts from the remainder). Polybius is a more perceptive analyst than Livy; and unlike Livy, he was both a contemporary and a Greek, who took part in some of the events he describes. Indeed, as a rising politician in the leading Achaean city of Megalopolis, he was one of those deported to Italy as hostages in 167, but he was held at Rome itself, where he became part of the circle surrounding the powerful Scipio family. This allowed him to see Roman decision-making from very near its centre; and it is the fact that he wrote to help his fellow-Greeks understand the growth of Roman imperial power that makes his work so illuminating.

One example of this may suffice. We saw at the end of chapter 1 that by the time of Aristotle (c. 330 BC), ancient political theorists were seeking to construct the ideal of a 'mixed' constitution – a blend of monarchy, oligarchy (or 'aristocracy'), and democracy – and to make their analysis of Sparta match this ideal. Aristotle's reaction (cited in ch. 1) had been simply to object that the theory did not fit the Spartan facts. Polybius' response is more complex. For him, Sparta is a not quite successful attempt at a mixed constitution (6.3-10), that had worked well until Sparta had begun to expand its power outside the Peloponnese (6.48-50). It is the Romans, in his view, who have managed by trial and error to develop the ideal mixed constitution, and have thereby broken out of the cycle of decline to which constitutions are naturally subject (6.10, 6.57-8). What matters here is not the plausibility of the analysis (which is negligible), but the attempt to come to terms with the new phenomenon that is Rome within a framework of traditional Greek concepts: if military success is the product of an ideal constitution, then the impotence of Sparta since 371 BC should lead to the dethronement of the Spartan myth.

Polybius, however, remained an exceptional critic, perhaps because he was naturally unsympathetic to Sparta. Sparta under Kleomenes and Nabis had opposed the growing power of Megalopolis and the Achaean League within the Peloponnese. After the assassination of Nabis in 192 BC, the Achaean commander Philopoimen (Polybius' fellow-citizen, and one of his heroes) had annexed Sparta. In 188, Philopoimen is said specifically to have abolished the Spartan *agôgê* (educational system), which was not apparently restored until the break-up of the Achaean League in 146.

We have already seen (in ch. 6) that Spartan constitutional arrangements were changed by the revolution of Agis and Kleomenes. The dual monarchy was abolished and never revived; and although we hear of ephors and of a *gerousia* throughout the Roman period, there is some evidence that both types of office were elected annually – which was the typical pattern for the magistrates of a Hellenistic or Roman city, whereas members of the *gerousia* in Classical Sparta had been elected for life. Similarly, there are evident differences between the *agôgê* which was abolished in 188 and that which was restored or re-invented in 146: in particular, the revived *agôgê* was apparently confined to boys over the age of 14, unlike its predecessor which had begun at the age of 7. The change in institutions is reflected by a change in the nature of the evidence. Inscriptions, which in earlier periods had been very rare, are common from Roman Sparta: as if Sparta was on one level trying to represent itself as a typical, literate, Hellenistic *polis*, while at the same time retaining or exaggerating its distinctiveness by re-inventing its ancient institutions.

It is because of Philopoimen's abolition of the *agôgê* that we need to be wary of accepting unsupported statements made by writers in the Roman period like Plutarch (who is, unfortunately, one of our most detailed sources for the *agôgê*), especially when they claim that what they are describing is a genuine antique. Conservatism was part of the myth of Sparta, and the point of claiming that an institution has existed unchanged since antiquity may be precisely to legitimate change. Indeed, how much anybody at Sparta in 146 knew about the pre-188 *agôgê* may be open to doubt, particularly given Sparta's traditional reliance on oral rather than written memory – a reliance which is reflected in the absence of Classical inscriptions.

This, however, did not bother the tourists, both Romans and Greeks from other *poleis*, who flocked to Sparta during the Roman period. What

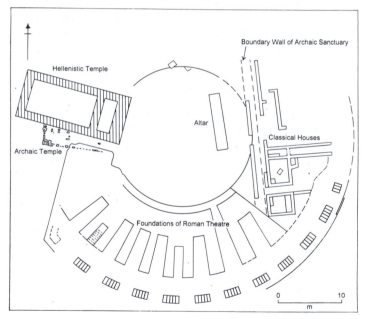

Fig. 19 Plan of the Sanctuary of Artemis Orthia at Sparta. [The temple and the altar were both in roughly the same place since the Archaic period, but the foundations of the original boundary wall and the houses outside it (probably fifth century BC) suggest that the building of the Roman theatre involved significantly extending the boundaries of the sanctuary.]

they were looking for was not accurate antiquarian scholarship, but the reconstruction of an ancient heritage of the type that today finds its place in a theme park. And just as such theme parks boost the local economy by providing employment to those willing to dress up in period costumes, so too there is evidence of Spartan readiness to meet the demands of the tourist trade.

One example of this adaptation to the tourist industry can be seen in the language of Spartan inscriptions. The Archaic and Classical Greek world had been one of separate dialects. Doric Greek, as spoken at Sparta and throughout most of the Peloponnese, was significantly different (especially in its vowel forms) from the Attic dialect with which modern readers are familiar from Athens. From the Hellenistic period, however, there is a growing tendency for inscriptions even from Doric cities to be written in what came to be known as *koinê* (lit. the 'common' dialect, originally derived from Attic). Inscriptions from Roman Sparta, on the other hand, are typically written in Doric. However, these texts sometimes insert the characteristic Doric vowels into words in which genuine Doric dialects had never used them. This suggests that the function of the dialect in these inscriptions is similar to that of Ye Olde Tea Shoppe: deliberate and not always accurate archaism, intended to create an atmosphere of spurious authenticity.

A more complex adaptation may perhaps be visible in the rituals surrounding the *agôgê*. Xenophon (*Lak.Pol.* 2.9), writing in the fourth century BC, speaks of a contest at the sanctuary of Artemis Orthia, in which Spartan boys tried to steal as many cheeses as possible from the altar, while others defended it with whips: evidently the aim for those running the gauntlet was to move so quickly that they got hit as little as possible. Various sources from the Roman period refer to what is evidently the same ritual (or at least a reconstruction of it), because it similarly took place at the altar of Artemis Orthia and involved the whipping of teenage Spartan boys. There is, however, a significant difference. None of these later sources mention cheeses, and they all imply that what is taking place is simply an endurance test – it is notable that the inscriptions from the Roman period refer to this as the *karterias agôn* or 'contest of endurance' – in which the aim is to sustain in silence as many blows as possible. It is probably an exaggeration when Plutarch (*Lycurgus* 18) claims to have seen 'many' competitors allowing themselves to be flogged to death, but the fact that Plutarch claims to have seen it is significant, because other writers also claim to have been present, and the layout of the sanctuary is suggestive. Excavations show a succession of temples and of altars from the Archaic period onwards, and a theatre of Roman date – as if deliberate attempts were being made to accommodate voyeuristic tourists to Sparta's high-class version of gladiatorial games.

The successful marketing of Sparta can be seen in a passage from the historian Cassius Dio. When Augustus, the first Roman emperor, visited Greece in 21 BC, he was already well-disposed to the Spartans for having provided sanctuary to Livia (whom he had since married) at a moment of crisis during the civil wars. Augustus rewarded the Spartans in an interesting way:

> He honoured them by giving them Kythera and by attending their *sussitia*.
>
> (Cassius Dio, 54.7.2)

Kythera was an island which had belonged to Sparta in the distant past, and its restoration was a mark of prestige as well as a territorial grant. Dining together in the *sussition*, however, had been an essential feature of the social system of Classical Sparta. The Spartans were 'honoured' by Augustus' attendance, because it gave imperial recognition to this reconstructed traditional activity.

Athens as University Town

The passage from Cassius Dio which was quoted at the end of the previous section continues in a way that emphasises the risks faced by Greek cities which supported the losing side (or supported the winning side but with insufficient enthusiasm) in disputes between or within the great powers. Athens had rather a poor record in picking winners in the first century BC. It had been used as a base by a supporter of Mithridates of Pontos, and following a siege, the city had been sacked in 86 BC by the Roman general Sulla. The Athenians had been contemptuously forgiven by Julius Caesar in the first phase of the civil wars, after supporting Pompey at the battle of Pharsalos (48 BC). At the battle of Actium (31 BC), in the final phase of the civil wars, the Athenians had once again backed a loser, this time Augustus' opponent Antony, and had paid the penalty:

> [Augustus] took away Aegina and Eretria, places which they had previously owned, and also forbade them to make anybody a citizen for money.
>
> (Cassius Dio, 54.7.2)

The last part of this sentence is interesting, because it hints at the Athenians' achievement in marketing their city as a different type of tourist attraction: a finishing school for young Roman aristocrats. The

Roman orator Cicero wrote a number of philosophical dialogues modelled on those of Plato. In Cicero's dialogues, however, the participants are typically Cicero and his aristocratic Roman friends rather than Socrates. The dialogues which make up the *De Finibus*, for instance, are set in Athens: the dramatic context of book 5 is an afternoon walk taken by Cicero as a young man after a morning spent attending a lecture; and the theme of the opening sections of this dialogue is whether it is more moving to read the great works of literature (which in context must mean Greek and specifically Athenian literature), or to visit the places hallowed by their association with Pericles and Demosthenes.

For a high-status Roman like Cicero, growing up in the early part of the first century BC, Athens was typically where one completed one's studies before returning to Rome to begin a political career. But a close friend of Cicero's, who became his most regular correspondent, decided to remain at Athens. Indeed, he lived there for the rest of his life and as a result is regularly known by the nickname 'Atticus' (i.e., 'the Athenian'). Atticus became in many ways more Athenian than the Athenians: his benefactions towards the city were such that he was offered honorary Athenian citizenship (but rejected it because of a legal quibble). Since the Classical period, the Athenians had had a tradition of granting citizenship to wealthy and distinguished foreign benefactors. What Cassius Dio's words imply is Augustus' perception that there were in some cases more crudely mercenary motives, with citizenship being offered in return for straight cash payments.

Whatever Augustus' initial feelings towards Athens, his anger soon cooled sufficiently for his close friend and son-in-law Agrippa to fund a substantial programme of public building there. The impact of this building programme can be most clearly seen in the *agora*, where the development of the site over time is particularly striking. The term *agora* denotes the market place and/or civic centre of a Greek *polis*, and at Athens our image is of a square open space marked out on each side by stoas (porticoes) set at right angles to each other. In fact, as fig. 20a reveals, the *agora* in the Classical period had relatively few stoas, and these did not serve to mark out the boundaries of the square: the Royal Stoa (rebuilt after 480 BC), the Poikile Stoa (built c. 460), and the Stoa of Zeus (c. 430) were all clustered around one corner of the *agora*, and even the South Stoa (c. 420) filled only half of one side of the square. The Classical *agora*, therefore, was a square open space surrounded by houses – or at least, a space that was capable of being open, because we should not forget the temporary presence of market stalls.

It was during the Hellenistic period that the *agora* was marked out by stoas around the perimeters of the square. The new South Stoa, the Middle Stoa, and the Stoa of Attalos were all built around 150 BC. It is the second and third of these which mark out two full sides of the *agora*, and highlight its characteristic shape (fig. 20b). Under Augustus, however, there were significant developments within the square. Two buildings in particular may be noted. The temple of Ares from Acharnae (outside the city) was demolished and rebuilt not along one of the sides of the *agora*, but protruding into it. There may be a connection here with the problems of succession within the imperial family (Gaius, the emperor's grandson and heir, was proclaimed as the 'new Ares' on a visit to Athens in 2 BC). Although this was an Athenian temple, its presence was a symbol of Roman rule. Even more significant, because of its size and its height, is the Odeion of Agrippa, a hall for concerts or lectures. This was constructed in front of the Middle Stoa, in such a way that it stretched nearly half way across the *agora* (fig. 20c). The impact of these changes is clear: whereas the Classical and even the Hellenistic *agora* had been an open place in which citizens could meet, the *agora* in

20 [a]   **1** Poikile Stoa   **2** Royal Stoa   **3** Stoa of Zeus   **4** South Stoa

20 [b]   **1** Stoa of Attalos   **2** Middle Stoa   **3** New South Stoa

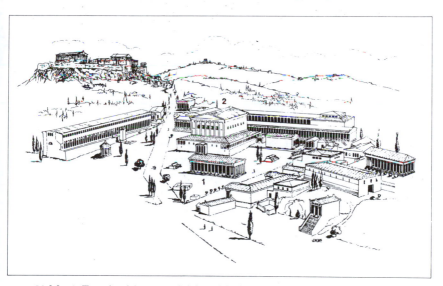

20 [c]   **1** Temple of Ares   **2** Odeion of Agrippa

Fig. 20 The Athenian *Agora* [a] c. 400 BC, [b] c. 150 BC, [c] c. 150 AD. [Each of these drawings shows the same site from the same angle (looking from the south-east, along the Street of the Panathenaic Procession towards the Acropolis). Only those buildings named in the text are identified.]

future was to be a place in which to look at monumental architecture symbolizing Roman rule.

Perhaps the most notable patron of Athens was the emperor Hadrian (AD 117-138), who also twice visited Sparta. He was the person who completed the building of the largest of Athenian temples, which is still the most massive of Athenian ruins: the temple of Olympian Zeus. This was a temple which had begun to be built more than six hundred years previously by the family of the tyrant Peisistratos, and which had remained incomplete since the expulsion of the tyranny (c. 510 BC). From one point of view, it was an unparalleled achievement to complete such a task. From another perspective, however, it could be seen as tactless to associate yourself too closely with a building originally begun by the tyrants: we may wonder whether Hadrian failed to see this point, or whether he simply did not care.

One of the most enigmatic monuments at Athens is the Arch of Hadrian, which stands close to one corner of the precinct of the temple of Olympian Zeus. The Arch carries an inscription on front and back, referring to Athens on one side as the city of Theseus (the mythical founder of the city) and on the other as the city of Hadrian. Scholars have traditionally seen this as evidence that Hadrian extended the city, on the assumption that it marks a boundary between the original city and an assumed new, Hadrianic quarter. However, it is linguistically easier to read not 'the ancient city of Theseus' but 'the former city of Theseus', and it has recently been argued that the Arch constitutes a claim that it is Hadrian and no longer Theseus who is the real founder of Athens.

Despite appearances, the final illustration in this book is not the Arch of Hadrian at Athens. It is one of a number of copies of Athenian monuments constructed on the estate of the Anson family (later Earls of Lichfield) at Shugborough in Staffordshire, following the work of the pioneering British antiquarians James Stuart and Nicholas Revett. Stuart and Revett stayed in Athens in 1751-1753, and were the first people to make architecturally detailed drawings of ancient buildings. Their visit was funded by the London Society of Dilettanti, which published the drawings. This publication was an important event in the history of modern attitudes to ancient Greece: it is partly because of Stuart and Revett that people today still go to Greece to look round ancient monuments; and it is partly because of their drawings that we still tend to look at ancient Greek art through eighteenth-century eyes.

Fig. 21 The Triumphal Arch at Shugborough. [Modelled on the Arch at Athens, and built in the 1760s under the direction of James 'Athenian' Stuart.]

This book has been focused from the outset around the idea that the history of Athens and of Sparta is a history of images. Stuart and Revett may provide a suitable point at which to conclude, because their work suggests that one reason why these two *poleis* are important is because of the images of Athens (or for that matter of Sparta) that people have constructed.

Suggestions for Further Study

1. The Ideal City?

Does Sparta deserve its current bad press, or is this simply the legacy of the way in which the image of Sparta has been used e.g. for the purposes of Nazi propaganda in the 1930s and 1940s?

It would now be technologically possible to reintroduce direct democracy (e.g. by televised debate followed immediately by electronic referendum), but few people seriously advocate doing this: why do you think this is so, and what implications does it have for our attitude to Athenian democracy?

2. Imperial Geography.

What political functions could be served by the control of a particular hero-cult in ancient Greece? Why did Cleisthenes of Sikyon borrow the cult of the Theban hero Melanippos (Herodotus 5.67-68), and why did Kimon discover the alleged bones of Theseus (Plut. *Theseus* 36 and *Kimon* 8)?

Nobody now believes in Athens as trading empire (i.e., markets for goods), but there is clear evidence that empire served as source for certain raw materials. How far was Athenian imperialism motivated by demand for food (evidenced by alleged sixth-century land-hunger), and how far was kicking other people around a sufficient motive in itself?

3. Democracy and Oligarchy.

Athenian lawcourts seem to spend a lot of time judging cases that are politically important, and the political power of the Spartan *gerousia* seems to depend largely on its status as a court. Why are lawcourts so political in the ancient Greek world?

How different was Athenian democracy in the fourth century from what it had been in the late fifth century?

Elections at Sparta are said to have been conducted not by counting votes but by estimating the volume of shouts from supporters of rival candidates, a method which Aristotle (*Politics* 2.9 = 1271a10) describes as 'childish'. So why did the Spartans do it?

4. *Life and Death.*

How effective was the Spartan attempt to promote loyalty to the group over loyalty to the family?

To what extent did the aristocratic symposium at Athens seek to promote class-loyalty over loyalty to the *polis*?

Spartan women are portrayed in our Athenian sources as being physically powerful and rather too loose in their behaviour. How do you think Spartan women would have regarded their Athenian counterparts?

5. *Thucydides and the War.*

Thucydides reports both Pericles (2.63) and Kleon (3.37) as saying to an Athenian assembly that their 'empire is like (or simply "is") a tyranny'. Bearing in mind the controversy surrounding the speeches in Thucydides, what if anything do these remarks tell us about Pericles, about Kleon, and about Thucydides?

What do you make of the relative reliability of Thucydides' and the *Ath.Pol.*'s accounts of the revolution of the Four Hundred, and what effect does this have on our perception of the rest of Thucydides' account (for which there is no alternative source)?

6. *Land Fit for Heroes?*

Why did Athens recover so quickly from losing the Peloponnesian War, and why did the power of Sparta decline so unexpectedly in the fourth century?

Are revolutionaries always people who seek to restore the past – and are people who seek to restore the past always revolutionaries?

7. *Greece under Roman Rule.*

In what ways is Plutarch's approach to the subjects of his Greek *Lives* conditioned by the political and intellectual background against which he was writing?

Would we be studying the history of Classical Greece if it had not been for Augustus, Hadrian, and the Roman Empire?

Suggestions for Further Reading

Ancient Texts available in Penguin Classics:

Aristophanes, *Knights and Other Plays* (includes *Birds* and *Wealth*).
Aristophanes, *Lysistrata and Other Plays* (includes *Acharnians*).
Aristotle, *Athenian Constitution* (abbreviated as '*Ath.Pol.*').
Aristotle, *Politics*.
Herodotus, *Histories*.
Livy, *Rome and the Mediterranean*.
Pausanias, *Guide to Greece*, 2 vols. (abbreviated as 'Pausan.').
Plutarch, *Age of Alexander* (abbreviated as 'Plut.') (includes *Lysander* and *Agesilaos*).
Plutarch, *Rise and Fall of Athens* (includes *Solon* and *Pericles*).
Plutarch on Sparta (includes *Lycurgus, Agis and Kleomenes*, and the *Sayings of Spartans* and *Sayings of Spartan Women*).
Polybius, *Rise of the Roman Empire* (selections only).
Thucydides, *Peloponnesian War* (abbreviated as 'Thuc.').
Xenophon, *History of My Times* (abbreviated as 'Xen. *Hell.*', i.e., *Hellênika*).

Other Ancient Texts cited in this book:

Book 54 of Cassius Dio's *Roman History* is translated in J. W. Rich, *Cassius Dio: The Augustan Settlement* (Aris & Phillips, 1990)

For Cicero's philosophical works, and for Diodoros, it is best to use the Loeb edition with facing translation. The same applies for pseudo-Demosthenes and pseudo-Plutarch (in each case printed in the Loeb among the genuine works of the appropriate author).

Xenophon, *Constitution of the Spartans* (abbreviated as 'Xen. *Lak.Pol.*'), is translated as an appendix to the Penguin *Plutarch on Sparta* (above), or alternatively in J.M. Moore, *Aristotle and Xenophon on Democracy and Oligarchy* (Chatto & Windus, 1975).

Pseudo-Xenophon (= The Old Oligarch), *Constitution of the Athenians* (abbreviated as '[Xen.] *Ath.Pol.*'), is translated in Moore (above), or in LACTOR (= London Association of Classical Teachers Original Records), vol. 2.

Selections of fragmentary texts (e.g. Tyrtaios, inscriptions) can be found in the series *Translated Documents of Greece and Rome*: C.W. Fornara, *Archaic Times to the End of the Peloponnesian War* (for the period down to 403), and P. Harding, *From the End of the Peloponnesian War to the Battle of Ipsus* (for the fourth century).

Modern Writers

1. The Ideal City?

Ethnicity (what it meant to be a Greek, or sometimes an Athenian) is an important theme in recent scholarship: see especially E.M. Hall, *Inventing the Barbarian: Greek Self-Definition through Tragedy* (Cambridge, 1989), and P.A. Cartledge, *The Greeks: a Portrait of Self and Other* (Oxford, 1993).

The image of Sparta has attracted attention since Ollier's *Le Mirage Spartiate* in the 1930s (never translated): of works in English, E.N. Tigerstedt, *The Legend of Sparta in Classical Antiquity* (2 vols., Stockholm, 1965-74) covers Greek and Roman views of Sparta; E. Rawson, *The Spartan Tradition in European Thought* (Oxford, 1969) extends the story down to Nazi Germany and beyond.

A wide-ranging introduction to the politics, culture, etc., of Classical Athens is JACT (= Joint Association of Classical Teachers), *The World of Athens* (Cambridge, 1984).

Several topics touched on in this chapter, and throughout the book, are the subject of separate volumes in the BCP Classical World series: see especially M. Baldock, *Greek Tragedy: an Introduction* (1989), P.A. Cartledge, *Aristophanes and his Theatre of the Absurd* (1990), N.R.E. Fisher, *Slavery in Classical Greece* (1993), R. Garland, *Religion and the Greeks* (1994), and J. Sharwood Smith, *Greece and the Persians* (1989).

2. Imperial Geography.

The best study of the physical remains of Archaic and Classical Sparta is J.T. Hooker, *The Ancient Spartans* (Dent, 1980), which concentrates particularly on archaeology and art history. On Athenian imperial buildings, see R.E. Wycherley, *The Stones of Athens* (Princeton, 1978).

P.A. Cartledge, *Sparta and Lakonia: a Regional History, 1300-362 BC* (Routledge, 1979), discusses the rise of Sparta; on the early development of the Peloponnesian League, and much else, see G.E.M. de Ste Croix, *The Origins of the Peloponnesian War* (Duckworth, 1972). On Athenian imperialism, R. Meiggs, *The Athenian Empire* (Oxford,

1972) remains fundamental, and despite the mass of detail it is extremely readable. Also useful is the first volume of the LACTOR (= London Association of Classical Teachers Original Records) sourcebooks, entitled *The Athenian Empire*: the third edition (1984) contains valuable interpretative essays by S. Hornblower and by J. K. Davies. Davies' own *Democracy and Classical Greece* (Fontana, ed.[2], 1993) is good on what can be done with inscriptions.

More technical, but wide-ranging, is P.D.A. Garnsey & C.R. Whittaker, eds, *Imperialism in the Ancient World* (Cambridge, 1978), which includes essays by Andrewes on Sparta and Finley on Athens.

3. Democracy and Oligarchy.

The study of Athenian democracy has been revolutionized since 1975 by M.H. Hansen. In particular, he has shown that the changes after the democratic restoration of 403/2 mean we can no longer (like earlier scholars) infer fifth-century practice from the relatively plentiful fourth-century sources. Of Hansen's two books, *The Athenian Democracy in the Age of Demosthenes: Structure, Principles and Ideology* (Blackwell, 1991) is more wide-ranging in its scope, but *The Athenian Assembly in the Age of Demosthenes* (Blackwell, 1987) has the advantage of giving the reader more direct access to the evidence and the arguments, and also of making clear in a very useful summary of conclusions which of Hansen's own views are now generally accepted and which are still contentious. For an independent post-Hansen synthesis, see R.K. Sinclair, *Democracy and Participation in Athens* (Cambridge, 1988). On specific topics, there are some interesting essays by M.I. Finley: try 'Athenian Demagogues' (in Finley's *Democracy Ancient and Modern*, Hogarth, 1985) on political leadership, and 'The Ancestral Constitution' (in his *Use and Abuse of History*, Hogarth, 1986) on the implications of the propaganda of 411 BC.

The most accessible detailed treatment of Spartan constitutional history is W.G. Forrest, *A History of Sparta* (Duckworth, ed.[2], 1980), but it is to my mind over-optimistic on the possibility of understanding early Sparta. Finley's essay on 'Sparta' (in his *Economy and Society in Ancient Greece*, Penguin, 1981), on the other hand, explicitly refuses to consider the early period and concentrates instead on the system as it existed in the fifth and fourth centuries. A.H.M. Jones, *Sparta* (Blackwell, 1967) still has a lot to offer on the government of Classical Sparta.

4. Life and Death.

On Greek religion, see L. Bruit Zaidman & P. Schmitt Pantel, *Religion in the Ancient Greek City* (Eng. trans., Cambridge, 1992). On Spartan and Athenian religion specifically, interesting contrasts (and parallels) are drawn by R. Parker's essay in A. Powell, ed., *Classical Sparta: the Techniques Behind her Success* (Routledge, 1989, useful also on what little is known about helot and perioikic cults).

Important contributions to our understanding of Spartan society are made in a series of papers by S.J. Hodkinson, especially in *Classical Quarterly*, 1986, pp. 378-406 on the rules of inheritance, and in *Chiron*, 1983, pp. 239-81 on the *agôgê*.

For rituals of growing-up at Athens, see P. Vidal-Naquet, 'The Black Hunter' and 'Recipes for Greek Adolescence' in R.L. Gordon, ed., *Greek Religion and Society* (Cambridge, 1981).

G. Clarke, *Women in the Ancient World* (*Greece & Rome New Surveys*, no. 21, ed.², 1993) is a good introduction to women in antiquity. For seclusion as a social code, try D. Cohen, 'The Social Context of Adultery at Athens', in P.A. Cartledge *et al*, eds, *Nomos* (Cambridge, 1990). On citizenship, autochthony, and the division of the sexes, see N. Loraux, *The Children of Athena* (Princeton, 1993).

On metics, there is nothing to rival D. Whitehead's pamphlet, *The Ideology of the Athenian Metic* (Cambridge Philological Society, 1977). There is a good introductory treatment of slaves at Athens (and of helots at Sparta) in Fisher's volume in this series (cf. above on ch. 1). M.I. Finley, 'Between Slavery and Freedom' (in his *Economy and Society*, cf. above on ch. 3) includes a series of essays on slavery and helots. For a survey (with bibliography) of the dispute on the use of slaves in Athenian agriculture, see either Fisher or else A. Burford, *Land and Labor in the Greek World* (Johns Hopkins, 1993).

5. Thucydides and the War.

On Thucydides, M.I. Finley's preface to the Penguin is good; the best detailed introduction is S. Hornblower, *Thucydides* (Duckworth, 1987). Those who wish to explore the rival accounts of the revolution of the Four Hundred offered by Thucydides and by the *Ath.Pol.* will find particularly useful the Penguin translation of the latter, which has excellent notes by P.J. Rhodes.

On the causes of the Peloponnesian War, the works cited in the text are Ste Croix, *Origins of the Peloponnesian War* (cf. above on ch. 2), a book of far greater breadth than might be suggested by its title, which deserves to be consulted on a wide range of issues of Athenian and Spartan imperialism, policy, and politics (there is a wealth of material stored in the appendices); and D. Kagan, *The Outbreak of the Peloponnesian War* (Cornell, 1969), the first part of his four-volume history of the War itself.

Two recent narrative histories of the fifth century are S. Hornblower, *The Greek World, 479-323 BC* (Routledge, ed.[3] 1993), which deals with the fourth century also and emphasizes the role of *poleis* other than Athens and Sparta; and A. Powell, *Athens and Sparta* (Routledge, 1988), good at leading students through the problems of the sources rather than telling them the answers.

On the techniques and logistics of ancient warfare, see generally V.D. Hanson, *The Western Way of War: Infantry Battle in Classical Greece* (Oxford, 1989) on hoplites, and on triremes J.S. Morrison & J.F. Coates, *The Athenian Trireme: the History and Reconstruction of an Ancient Greek Warship* (Cambridge, 1986).

6. Land Fit for Heroes?

An important treatment of fourth-century Spartan society (and much else) is P.A. Cartledge, *Agesilaos and the Crisis of Sparta* (Duckworth, 1987). For Sparta's relationships with Persia during the late fifth and early fourth centuries, see D.M. Lewis, *Sparta and Persia* (Leiden, 1977). The diplomatic dealings surrounding the peace of 387, and later common peaces, are examined exhaustively in T. Ryder, *Koine Eirene* (Oxford, 1965).

Fourth-century Athens has been a growth-area in recent scholarship, mainly because of the insistence of scholars working on political history that our relatively plentiful fourth-century sources on Athenian democracy are sources for fourth- rather than for fifth-century democracy (note the way in which both the works of Hansen cited on ch. 3 above are explicitly about Demosthenic rather than Periclean Athens). Euboulos and Lycurgus, by contrast, have received relatively little attention: the most recent treatment of the former is in a paper by G. Cawkwell in *Journal of Hellenic Studies*, 1963, pp. 47-67, and of the latter by F.W. Mitchel in *Lycurgan Athens* (Cincinnati, 1970). On the extent to which Athenians during this period knew about their past, see R. Thomas, *Oral Tradition and Written Record in Classical Athens* (Cambridge, 1989). The change from liturgies to euergetism in the Hellenistic and Roman world is explored in a provocative book by P. Veyne, *Bread and Circuses* (Eng. trans., Allen Lane, 1990).

For Sparta in the Hellenistic period, there is nothing to rival P.A. Cartledge & A. Spawforth, *Hellenistic and Roman Sparta* (Routledge, 1989).

7. Roman Greece.

S. Alcock, *Graecia Capta* (Cambridge, 1993), is an important general treatment of Roman Greece, which is good on settlement patterns and the construction of civic space. For Roman views of Greeks (and Greek views of Romans) as expressed in our literary sources, there is much of value in J.P.V.D. Balsdon, *Romans and Aliens* (Duckworth, 1979).

The concept of Sparta as a theme park is borrowed from an article entitled 'Sparta: the World's First Heritage Centre', in *Current Archaeology*, 1992, pp. 432-7, which is a good starting point. The second half of Cartledge & Spawforth (cf. on ch. 6 above) offers more detail on Roman Sparta. For the image of Sparta during this period, see the Roman chapters of Tigerstedt and of Rawson (cf. on ch. 1 above).

Two useful studies of the Athenian *agora* are H. Thompson & R.E. Wycherley, *The Agora of Athens* (American School of Classical Studies at Athens, 1972), and J.M. Camp, *The Athenian Agora: Excavations in the Heart of Classical Athens* (Thames & Hudson, 1986). On the work of Stuart (and Revett), see D. Watkin, *'Athenian' Stuart, Pioneer of the Greek Revival* (Allen & Unwin, 1982).

3 5282 00436 5345